# The Greatest Hunting Dog Stories Ever Told

## Edited by Lamar Underwood

LYONS
PRESS

*Guilford, Connecticut*

An imprint of Globe Pequot, the trade division of
The Rowman & Littlefield Publishing Group, Inc.
4501 Forbes Blvd., Ste. 200
Lanham, MD 20706
www.rowman.com

Distributed by NATIONAL BOOK NETWORK

British Library Cataloguing in Publication Information available

**Library of Congress Cataloging-in-Publication Data**

Names: Underwood, Lamar, editor.
Title: The greatest hunting dog stories ever told / edited by Lamar Underwood.
Description: Guilford, Connecticut: Lyons Press, [2021] | Summary: "An unparalleled collection of
   the finest writings about hunting dogs"—Provided by publisher.
Identifiers: LCCN 2021021708 | ISBN 9781493058532 (trade paperback)
Subjects: LCSH: Hunting dogs—United States—Anecdotes.
Classification: LCC SF428.5.G74 2021 | DDC 636.750973--dc23
LC record available at https://lccn.loc.gov/2021021708

♾️™ The paper used in this publication meets the minimum requirements of American National
Standard for Information Sciences—Permanence of Paper for Printed Library Materials, ANSI/
NISO Z39.48-1992.

# CONTENTS

# CONTENTS

# INTRODUCTION

MY BRETHREN OF THE CHASE WITH ROD OR GUN HAVE NEVER OUT-grown a couple of standard cliches to hide their disappointment of those days when nary a fin nor feather was encountered. Blank days for the diary or calendar. No strikes, not even nibbles from invisible fish. No flushes or glimpses of birds. A lot of casts and tramping the woods without anything to take home.

Anglers come out of this funk chirping a favorite song: "Oh well, it was great just being out there."

The hunter with nothing in his bird vest except unused shells will probably say, "Oh well, I loved watching the dogs work."

"Watching the dogs work" has been an expression this hunter has used countless times in many years of watching bird dogs and retrievers go about their business on days destined to be fruitless. Sometimes on those days moments of elation occurred, like the heart-stopping sight of my pointer hitting a scent trail, pausing, then creeping nose-down into the tangled brush bordering the field. When the scent seemed to wane, the dog's circling, scouting motions failed to locate birds. Perhaps a covey had been busted by a hawk here. Who knows? The scoreboard still had a big fat zero on it.

Don't be fooled by the smile and familiar words, "I loved watching the dogs work." Behind those words lurks a cloud of disappointment that no pretended enthusiasm can change. When this kind of thing happens a lot, doubts about one's bird dog drift in like a cold fog. Keep a bird dog year-around, love it with all your heart, and you'll find that "watching the dogs work" is a poor substitute for finding birds, shooting hits and misses, and a dog's muzzle holding a bird for your hand every now and then.

In the pages ahead, the dogs you'll go afield with are very seldom going to disappoint. There may be a flushed bird or two, a lost hound, a flat refusal to pick up a bird lying in plain sight—maladies of any hunt but only temporary setbacks. These are dogs with performances in the field that deserve to be pointed out.

Whether his dog lives in a concrete run behind a chain-link fence or on a rug beside the fireplace, the true dog man will have no boundaries to the love he feels. Bumped birds, refusals to retrieve, runaway high jinks—all can be forgiven if the dog occasionally shows glimpses of what can happen: scent trails unraveled, solid points, retrieves that can be remembered and bragged about to friends.

Dog owners, I'm forced by experience to admit, sometimes suffer from lack of experience. The pointing dog owner may have never seen a top-notch setter, pointer, or Brittany in the field. The way a dog works the fields and cover, finds scent and then locks up into a statue-like point, backs the points of other dogs, retrieves with eagerness right to your hand, keeps in touch with the gunner: all these ingredients of the hunt don't have to be handled to perfection, and probably won't be, but the dog that can "do it all" (as proclaimed in *American Field* advertisements) will make you a proud owner.

How about steady to wing and shot? you might ask. If you are interested in taking home trophies from field trials, the requirement is definitely in place. Most gun dog owners don't train that hard.

The hard training of field trial dogs reaches a pinnacle with training on the Canadian prairie country. In late summer, the best (and most expensive) dog trainers take their charges to the open reaches of country where they work with sharptail grouse and other birds available in great numbers in good years. By the time field trials and gunning activities start, the dogs are ready for high-powered performances. So high-powered, in fact, that hunting these dogs requires big country—so big that the dogs can hunt in racehorse-like strides that cover many acres before you can get the words "Hunt close!" out of your mouth. There are places of big fields where this kind of hunting is still possible. Sometimes these dogs are followed on horseback or mule-driven wagons, and today's owners of big-going dogs might be following their pointers and setters in all-terrain vehicles, as their dogs become distant specks on the far ends of soybean fields.

For most of us serious bird hunters, perfection rests not on speed and distance, but in those choice words, "Hunt close." The dog that can work close to the gun in tight cover, such as New England hillsides, then bend on out a little as the fields open, as in Tennessee croplands—that's our dog!

My experiences with retrievers have not come from ownership, but from the good fortune of sharing waterfowl blinds with men like Gene Hill, Tom Hennessey, and many excellent guides. I've seen gallant dogs bring in birds that would have been lost had they not tackled the ordeals of weather, waves, and distances.

Although I've owned two pointers (trained one of them), I've never owned a Lab or Chessie. My only retriever was a flushing dog, a springer spaniel that for a while had me thinking I had the perfect gun dog. Jumper was trained by professionals and came to me with varsity skills. He hunted close enough to the gun so shots were possible on anything he pried loose from the cover. His nose-down, butt-shaking pursuit of scent took him deep into the tangles of brier and weeds where quail, pheasant, or rabbits were lurking. He did not point his birds, but when he sent them vaulting into flight, I had a decent shot. When I connected, my springer carried them to me with enthusiasm that I thought to be pride. Eventually, I was forced to move into cities and crowded living conditions, and my days with my springer ended. I never got around to owning another pointer.

Not so long ago I was looking at some old artwork depicting hunting scenes from medieval times. The setting was obviously a castle-like estate, and the hunting party was setting out with pointing dogs galore and retrievers, plus, bringing up the rear, a pack of yip-yapping spaniels. They were headed for a day of hunting fit for a king.

That's the way great gun dogs can make you feel, even today. Like you're a king.

—Lamar Underwood, Editor

*"I can't think of anything that brings me closer to tears than when my old dog—completely exhausted after a full and hard day in the field—limps away from her nice spot in front of the fire and comes over to where I'm sitting and puts her head in my lap, a paw over my knee, and closes her eyes and goes back to sleep. I don't know what I've done to deserve that kind of friend, but I'm humble enough not to ask any questions."*

—GENE HILL, TEARS AND LAUGHTER: A COUPLE OF DOZEN
DOG STORIES (PETERSEN PRINTS, LOS ANGELES, 1981).
SEE CHAPTER 2 OF THIS BOOK.

## Chapter 1

# The Road to Tinkhamtown

### By Corey Ford

*If you own a copy of the June 1970 issue of Field & Stream magazine, consider yourself lucky. That was the seventy-fifth anniversary issue, a fine thing. But that's not the reason that issue was so precious. Illustrated with a painting by Howard Terpning, Corey Ford's story "The Road to Tinkhamtown" makes that issue a classic. The editors prefaced it with this blurb: "This story by the late Corey Ford, here published for the first time anywhere, is a moving tale which will not soon be forgotten. It is for all those who mourned his death that we present this farewell from the creator of "The Lower Forty.'" A few months after he wrote this story, Ford (1902–1969) passed away. He never saw "Tinkhamtown" in print. Ford's stories and his "Lower Forty" column were Field & Stream favorites. His setters provided the background of many of his tales. "Tinkhamtown" was his masterpiece, written in the evening of his life, written with skill and love, a dog story unlike any other. More than any story I know, this one brings to mind the great William Faulkner quote: "The past is never dead. It's not even past."*

It was a long way, but he knew where he was going. He would follow the road through the woods and over the crest of a hill and down the hill to the stream, and cross the sagging timbers of the bridge, and on the other side would be the place called Tinkhamtown. He was going back to Tinkhamtown.

He walked slowly at first, his legs dragging with each step. He had not walked for almost a year, and his flanks had shriveled and wasted away from lying in bed so long; he could fit his fingers around his thigh. Doc Towle had said he would never walk again, but that was Doc for you, always on the pessimistic side. Why, now he was walking quite easily, once he had started. The strength was coming back into his legs, and he did not have to stop for breath so often. He tried jogging a few steps, just to show he could, but he slowed again because he had a long way to go.

It was hard to make out the old road, choked with alders and covered by matted leaves, and he shut his eyes so he could see it better. He could always see it when he shut his eyes. Yes, here was the beaver dam on the right, just as he remembered it, and the flooded stretch where he had picked his way from hummock to hummock while the dog splashed unconcernedly in front of him. The water had been over his boot tops in one place, and sure enough, as he waded it now his left boot filled with water again, the same warm squdgy feeling. Everything was the way it had been that afternoon, nothing had changed in ten years. Here was the blowdown across the road that he had clambered over, and here on a knoll was the clump of thorn apples where a grouse had flushed as they passed. Shad had wanted to look for it, but he had whistled him back. They were looking for Tinkhamtown.

He had come across the name on a map in the town library. He used to study the old maps and survey charts of the state; sometimes they showed where a farming community had flourished, a century ago, and around the abandoned pastures and in the orchards grown up to pine the birds would be feeding undisturbed. Some of his best grouse covers had been located that way. The map had been rolled up in a cardboard cylinder; it crackled with age as he spread it out. The date was 1857. It was the sector between Cardigan and Kearsarge Mountains, a wasteland of slash and second-growth timber without habitation today, but evidently it had supported a number of families before the Civil War. A road was marked on the map, dotted with X's for homesteads, and the names of the owners were lettered beside them: Nason J. Tinkham, Allard R. Tinkham. Half the names were Tinkham. In the center of the map—the paper was so yellow that he could barely make it out—was the word "Tinkhamtown."

He had a drawn a rough sketch on the back of an envelope, noting where the road left the highway and ran north to a fork and then turned east and crossed a stream that was not even named; and the next morning he and Shad had set out together to find the place. They could not drive very far in the jeep, because washouts had gutted the roadbed and laid bare the ledges and boulders. He had stuffed the sketch in his hunting-coat pocket and hung his shotgun over his forearm and started walking, the setter trotting ahead with the bell on his collar tinkling. It was an old-fashioned sleigh bell, and it had a thin silvery note that echoed through the woods like peepers in the spring. He could follow the sound in the thickest cover, and when it stopped he would go to where he heard it last and Shad would be on point. After Shad's death, he had put the bell away. He'd never had another dog.

It was silent in the woods without the bell, and the way was longer than he remembered. He should have come to the big hill by now. Maybe he'd taken the wrong turn back at the fork. He thrust a hand into his hunting coat; the envelope with the sketch was still in the pocket. He sat down on a flat rock to get his bearings, and then he realized, with a surge of excitement, that he had stopped on this very rock for lunch ten years ago. Here was the waxed paper from his sandwich, tucked in a crevice, and here was the hollow in the leaves where Shad had stretched out beside him, the dog's soft muzzle flattened on his thigh. He looked up, and through the trees he could see the hill.

He rose and started walking again, carrying his shotgun. He had left the gun standing in its rack in the kitchen when he had been taken to the state hospital, but now it was hooked over his arm by the trigger guard; he could feel the solid heft of it. The woods grew more dense as he climbed, but here and there a shaft of sunlight slanted through the trees. "And there were forests ancient as the hills," he thought, "enfolding sunny spots of greenery." Funny that should come back to him now; he hadn't read it since he was a boy. Other things were coming back to him, the smell of dank leaves and sweet fern and frosted apples, the sharp contrast of sun and cool shade, the November stillness before snow. He walked faster feeling the excitement swell within him.

He paused on the crest of the hill, straining his ears for the faint mutter of the stream below him, but he could not hear it because of the voices. He wished they would stop talking, so he could hear the stream. Someone was saying his name over and over, "Frank, Frank," and he opened his eyes reluctantly and worried, and there was nothing to worry about. He tried to tell her where he was going, but when he moved his lips the words would not form. "What did you say, Frank?" she asked, bending her head lower. "I don't understand." He couldn't make the words any clearer, and she straightened and said to Doc Towle: "It sounded like Tinkhamtown."

"Tinkhamtown?" Doc shook his head, "Never heard him mention any place by that name."

He smiled to himself. Of course he'd never mentioned it to Doc. Things like a secret grouse cover you didn't mention to anyone, not even to as close a friend as Doc was. No, he and Shad were the only ones who knew. They found it together, that long ago afternoon, and it was their secret.

They had come to the stream—he shut his eyes so he could see it again—and Shad had trotted across the bridge. He had followed more cautiously, avoiding the loose planks and walking along a beam with his shotgun held out to balance himself. On the other side of the stream the road mounted steeply to a clearing in the woods, and he halted before the split-stone foundation of a house, the first of the series of farms shown on the map. It must have been a long time since the building had fallen in; the cottonwoods growing in the cellar hole were twenty, maybe thirty years old. His boot overturned a rusted axe blade, and the handle of a china cup in the grass; that was all. Beside the doorstep was a lilac bush, almost as tall as the cottonwoods. He thought of the wife who had set it out, a little shrub then, and the husband who had chided her for wasting time on such frivolous things with all the farmwork to be done. But the work had come to nothing, and still the lilac bloomed each spring, the one thing that had survived.

Shad's bell was moving along the stone wall at the edge of the clearing, and he strolled after him, not hunting, wondering about the people who had gone away and left their walls to crumble and their buildings to collapse under the winter snows. Had they ever come back to Tinkhamtown? Were they here now, watching him unseen? His toe stubbed against a block of hewn granite hidden by briers, part of the sill of the old barn. Once it had been a tight barn, warm with cattle steaming in their stalls, rich with the blend of hay and manure and harness leather. He liked to think of it the way it was; it was more real than this bare rectangle of blocks and the emptiness inside. He'd always felt that way about the past. Doc used to argue that what's over is over, but he would insist Doc was wrong. Everything is the way it was, he'd tell Doc. The past never changes. You leave it and go on to the present, but it is still there, waiting for you to come back to it.

He had been so wrapped in his thoughts that he had not realized Shad's bell had stopped. He hurried across the clearing holding his gun ready. In a corner of the stone wall an ancient apple tree had littered the ground with fallen fruit, and beneath it Shad was standing motionless. The white fan of his tail was lifted a little and his backline was level, the neck craned forward, one foreleg cocked. His flanks were trembling with the nearness of grouse, and a thin skein of drool hung from his jowls. The dog did not move as he approached, but the brown eyes rolled back until their whites showed, looking for him. "Steady, boy," he called. His throat was tight, the way it always got when Shad was on point, and he had to swallow hard. "Steady, I'm coming."

"I think his lips moved just now," his sister's voice said. He did not open his eyes, because he was waiting for the grouse to get up in front of Shad, but he knew Doc Towle was looking at him. "He's sleeping," Doc said after a moment. "Maybe you better get some sleep yourself, Mrs. Duncombe." He heard Doc's heavy footsteps cross the room. "Call me if there's any change," Doc said, and closed the door, and in the silence he could hear his sister's chair creaking beside him, her silk dress rustling regularly as she breathed.

What was she doing here, he wondered. Why had she come all the way from California to see him? It was the first time they had seen each other since she had married and moved out West. She was his only relative, but they had never been very close; they had nothing in common, really. He heard from her now and then, but it was always the same letter: Why didn't he sell the old place, it was too big for him now that the folks had passed on, why didn't he take a small apartment in town where he wouldn't be alone? But he liked the big house, and he wasn't alone, not with Shad. He had closed off all the other rooms and moved into the kitchen so everything would be handy. His sister didn't approve of his bachelor ways, but it was very comfortable with his cot by the stove and Shad curled on the floor near him at night, whinnying and scratching the linoleum with his claws as he chased a bird in a dream. He wasn't alone when he heard that.

He had never married. He had looked after the folks as long as they lived; maybe that was why. Shad was his family. They were always together—Shad was short for Shadow—and there was a closeness between them that he did not feel for anyone else, not his sister or Doc even. He and Shad used to talk without words, each knowing what the other was thinking, and they could always find one another in the woods. He still remembered the little things about him: the possessive thrust of his jaw, the way he false-yawned when he was vexed, the setter stubbornness sometimes, the clownish grin when they were going hunting, the kind eyes. That was it: Shad was the kindest person he had ever known.

They had not hunted again after Tinkhamtown. The old dog had stumbled several times, walking back to the jeep, and he had to carry him in his arms the last hundred yards. It was hard to realize he was gone. He liked to think of him the way he was; it was like the barn, it was more real than the emptiness. Sometimes at night, lying awake with the pain in his legs, he would hear the scratch of claws on the linoleum, and he would turn on the light and the hospital room would be empty. But when he turned the light off he would hear the scratching again, and he would be content and drop off to sleep, or what passed for sleep in these days and nights that ran together without dusk or dawn.

Once he asked Doc point-blank if he would ever get well. Doc was giving him something for the pain, and he hesitated a moment and finished what he was doing and cleaned the needle and then looked at him and said: "I'm afraid not, Frank." They had grown up in the town together, and Doc knew him too well to lie. "I'm afraid there's nothing to do." Nothing to do but lie there and wait till it was over. "Tell me, Doc," he whispered, for his voice wasn't very strong, "what happens when it's over?" And Doc fumbled with the catch of his black bag and closed it and said well he supposed you went on to someplace else called the Hereafter. But he shook his head: He always argued with Doc. "No, it isn't someplace else," he told him, "it's someplace you've been where you want to be again." Doc didn't understand, and he couldn't explain it any better. He knew what he meant, but the shot was taking effect and he was tried.

He was tired now, and his legs ached a little as he started down the hill, trying to find the stream. It was too dark under the trees to see the sketch he had drawn, and he could not tell direction by the moss on the north side of the trunks. The moss grew all around them, swelling them out of size, and huge blowdowns blocked his way. Their upended roots were black and misshapen, and now instead of excitement he felt a surge of panic. He floundered through a pile of slash, his legs throbbing with pain as the sharp points stabbed him, but he did not have the strength to get to the other side and he had to back out again and circle. He did not know where he was going. It was getting late, and he had lost the way.

There was no sound in the woods, nothing to guide him, nothing but his sister's chair creaking and her breath catching now and then in a dry sob. She wanted him to turn back, and Doc wanted him to, they all wanted him to turn back. He thought of the big house; if he left it alone it would fall in with the winter snows and cottonwoods would grow in the cellar hole. And there were all the other doubts, but most of all there was the fear. He was afraid of the darkness, and being alone, and not knowing where he was going. It would be better to turn around and go back. He knew the way back.

And then he heard it, echoing through the woods like peepers in the spring, the thin silvery tinkle of a sleigh bell. He started running toward it, following the sound down the hill. His legs were strong again, and he hurdled the blowdowns, he leapt over fallen logs, he put one fingertip on a pile of slash and sailed over it like a grouse skimming. He was getting nearer and the sound filled his ears, louder than a thousand church bells ringing, louder than all the choirs in the sky, as loud as the pounding of his heart. The fear was gone; he was not lost. He had the bell to guide him now.

He came to the stream, and paused for a moment at the bridge. He wanted to tell them he was happy, if they only knew how happy he was, but when he opened his eyes he could not see them anymore. Everything else was bright, but the room was dark.

The bell had stopped and he looked across the stream. The other side was bathed in sunshine, and he could see the road mounting steeply, and the clearing in the woods, and the apple tree in a corner of the stone wall.

Shad was standing motionless beneath it, the white fan of his tail lifted, his neck craned forward and one foreleg cocked. The whites of his eyes showed as he looked back. waiting for him.

"Steady," he called, "steady, boy." He started across the bridge. "I'm coming."

CHAPTER 2

# The Dog Man

By Gene Hill

*My late friend Gene Hill (1928–1997) loved hunting dogs like no other dog owner I've ever known. And he wrote about them in great prose that holds a reader hard with its clarity, honesty, and recognition of shared emotions. Beginning with* A Hunter's Fireside Book *and continuing through eleven other books, all stemming from his magazine articles, Gene's audience loved his stories. He was a dear friend who shared editorial reins with me at* Sports Afield, *where he did the "Mostly Tailfeathers" column, then went on to* Field & Stream *for the "Hill Country" column. Prior to* Sports Afield, *Gene did a column for* Guns & Ammo *magazine. This story is excerpted from Gene's book* Tears and Laughter: A Couple of Dozen Dog Stories (1981), *illustrated by Herb Strasser.*

The Dog Man smokes his pipe and walks around staring at the litter of puppies. Years of experience have prepared him for this moment. He can recite the conformation and peculiarities of every fine dog of the breed. His careful study of the lineage of the sire and the dam and their sires and dams is reflected in his perceptive eyes. He is cold and unemotional because he knows that shortly he is going to pick a gunning companion that will be at his side for years. One of these seven-week-old puppies today brawling with its kin in the pen will shortly, by his urging and handling, fuse all its great instincts into The Perfect Dog.

He reaches in and hefts several of the puppies. He lifts their ears and they sink their little needle teeth into his fingers. He reaches into his pocket and brings forth a carefully preserved grouse wing—saved from last fall for precisely this moment. He unwinds the fishing line he has wrapped around it and trolls it through the boiling orange and white sea in the pen. They leap on the grouse wing and shred it. The Dog Man is delighted.

The choice is difficult. Suddenly in the midst of his weighty speculation, he feels an acute pain in his ankle. A young setter bitch has crawled out of the pile and bitten him. He brushes her away and she worries his trouser cuff. The Dog Man is concentrating on a frisky male wrestling with one of his brothers in a corner. The little female puppy is now into his shoelaces. He picks her up and she licks his face and snuggles into his arms. She has chosen the Dog Man. The visions of the young male on point fade as he shifts the sleeping puppy from one arm to the other to pay the man who runs the kennel. All the way home the Dog Man drives very carefully because the pup has her head in his lap. His family, who has been waiting on the front lawn, watches as he holds up the pup and listens as he begins lecturing.

"This is a bird dog; an English Setter of the Laverack type. She is an orange Belton. She is not a toy nor is she to be a house pet. She is a hunting machine. She will live in the kennel."

Having made his speech the Dog Man puts the pup on the lawn and his family fondles it. An hour later the Dog Man is sitting in his study reading the chapter on puppies in *Gun Dog* for the fifteenth time. The puppy is asleep in his lap, stuffed to bursting with biscuits.

In six months the new doghouse is used to store kindling. The pup sleeps in the armchair in the Dog Man's bedroom. His clothes are covered with orange and white hair. All in the family sneak goodies to the dog under the dining room table. The Dog Man severely admonishes them for this, even while doing it himself.

As time goes by the Dog Man will have acquired, at the very least, a set of whistles, a flushing whip, a bell for the dog's collar, training dummies, tubes of so-called quail and pheasant scent, various combs, brushes, shampoos, sprays, ointments and an assortment of leashes and ropes. The old doorknobs will have been replaced by new ones bearing likenesses of pointing dogs and upland birds. Coffee cups will arrive bearing similar motifs. The reliable family sedan has given way to a fancy station wagon outfitted with an expensive kennel. An array of packages and bottles containing vitamins and various dietary supplements will stand near the prepared-dog-food bag (whose contents he knows by heart, right down to the percentage of carbohydrates and "fiber").

Expensive prints of dogs on point in Georgia, Alabama, Texas and the Carolinas will be arrayed on the walls. His wife will wonder why he never paid half that much attention to her or his children, but she will not say so out loud. She instinctively knows that a Dog Man does not have too much time in his life for trivial small talk. She will have to learn the difference between "breaking," "bolting" and "blinking."

If she needs a new winter coat she is more likely to get a pair of leather-faced brush pants and a matching canvas coat, two sizes too big, so she can attend field trials with him and look the part of the Dog Man's wife. (The most important thing for a lady to know about field trials is that they are held in the open and that there is no bathroom.)

In brief, the Dog Man is not like ordinary sane men. He is a subspecies whose habitat, language, working patterns, familial relationships and drinking styles set him apart. Scientific studies have indicated that this condition is irreversible and that he tends to throw similarly minded offspring.

I must confess that I am the same sort: a Dog Man. Dogs of all sorts of breeds have selected me with the canny instinct that a con-man has for a sucker. They spot me as undisciplined, self-indulgent and addicted to indolence—in short, the perfect type of man for the average dog to own.

One of the problems afflicting the Dog Man is that despite his subscription to all the field-trial news magazines, avidly reading every dog book ever printed and even having a fairly wide range of shooting experiences, chances are he seldom has the opportunity to see a really first-rate, fully schooled bird dog on the job and under his gun. He knows in theory what to expect but he rarely, if ever, has the blessed opportunity to be in on such a day in the field. The few relatively competent dogs that I've gunned over have trained themselves. Their owners claim to the contrary. A really good dog trainer is a man of infinite patience, understanding and skill. I'm convinced that more dogs are ruined by the lack of ability or knowledge and patience of a trainer to put himself in the position of the dog—literally and figuratively—than any other single thing.

And certain men have a way with certain kinds of dogs. My friend, Bill Wunderlich, is one of the finest professional trainers of retrievers. He knows how they are going to think before they do, and more often than not, Billy can anticipate a mistake and prevent it from happening, turning a possible negative experience into a positive one. To see him work a young dog is an awesome experience in human skill and understanding. Yet Billy has a great fondness for pointers and by his own admission really just can't seem to break one himself and buys his pointing dogs trained.

My advice on dog training is generally worth just about what it costs, but here it is anyway. Don't expect more from a dog than you're willing to put into working with him. And to find out how much work it really is, make a point of seeing a field trail and finding out what a first-class dog can do—and talk to the man who runs the dogs. If you can afford it, and I think it's the least expensive in the long run, and if you're really serious about having a good dog, you're ahead by buying one fully trained or at least well-started.

It takes a lot of time to do it yourself—and by a lot of time I mean virtually every single day that's possible should have some time allotted to working your dog. If you're willing to devote that much time, fine. You'll have one of the most rewarding experiences of your life. But I'm heavily oriented toward the professionals. If I had the time I'd start out by spending as much time with the pros as I could, and expect to pay them for their advice and help. Most of them have seen more and forgotten more about dogs than you or I will ever dream of. I've read everything I could, but it's one thing to study up on handling a Labrador on a blind retrieve and something else to see Billy Wunderlich actually do it. I believe that a dog likes to be good at what he's supposed to do, that they understand discipline as much as they understand affection and that the two should be ladled out freely.

I remember training one of my Labradors to do a rather difficult series of retrieves which involved going from land through water, over land and through water again to find a bird that she hadn't seen shot. Time and again she fell short of what I expected and both her patience and mine were beginning to fray a lot more than just around the edges.

Just about the time I began shouting like a maniac out of pure frustration, the dog came back to within a few feet of me and waited until I had calmed down and then, through the expression on her face, told me as plainly as if she could speak that she didn't really understand what I wanted her to do and that if I could find some way of explaining it, she'd be pleased to do it my way. And that's finally what happened.

Nelson Sills, whom I consider to be one of the finest trainers and judges of retrievers, once put it much more succinctly to me after watching me mishandle a dog that was clearly the best one in the trial he was judging. "Gene," he said, "it's too damn bad that you aren't nearly as good at handling as your dog is at retrieving." His implication, and it was true, was that if I'd left the dog alone that particular time she would have won. Too many dog owners don't know when to stay out of the act. When in doubt, don't do anything until you know what you're doing. If I had a nickel for every time I've called a bird dog off a near-point or given a retriever a bad line because I didn't understand what was going on, I could buy a dog that is smart enough not to pay attention to me when I'm making an ass out of myself.

Take the time to know your dog. I've got four in my kennel right now and every one is an individual and every one has to be handled according to its own peculiarities. (The same way my wife handles me according to my own idiosyncrasies.) Be plentiful in praise for their successes and slow to condemn their faults.

I can't conceive of hunting without a dog. I just don't enjoy a day in the field without seeing the fun that a dog has in working. If I have to choose between leaving the gun home or the dog, I'll set out with the dog.

When all is said and done, the things we remember most about our dogs are their oddities. And I can say with full knowledge that nobody will fully agree with me, that English Setters have done more to drive the Dog Man to the Jack Daniels jar than all the other breeds combined.

I once gave an English Setter puppy to my good friend, Bill Gray, the best veterinarian I know. Shelly instantly took over the good sofa, in spite of the lecture Bill gave his family and his initial intentions of establishing the mythical dog-master relationship. If Shelly were asleep on the sofa, shedding at a pretty good rate, everybody had to talk in a low voice and tip-toe around the room. I didn't understand why this was necessary because Shelly, like most dogs, was convinced that the ideal life was to sleep about 23 hours a day and reserve awake time for eating. Bill, of course, took her hunting and boasted constantly about Shelly's abilities as a woodcock dog in spite of the fact that Shelly never actually pointed the way dogs do in magazine illustrations. When she came up on a bird she'd just stop and stand there. I was convinced after seeing this that she was taking a little nap while Bill went about his business of flushing and shooting. In fact, this odd posture of hers was almost the undoing of Bill.

I met him on the street one day and asked him how Shelly was doing. "Just great," Bill said, and went down on his hands and knees in the street by my car to demonstrate how Shelly acted on a bird. He gave a perfect imitation, dropping his head down on his chest and closing his eyes and being so staunch that he came within an inch of being hit by a bread truck.

Even after a long year of force training, the only thing one of my English Setters would pick up without tortured reluctance was unbroken clay targets. Looking back on it, just this minute, I guess that's where she had the most opportunity.

Another little liver-and-white setter of mine was, not happily for me, completely convinced he could fly. I can see him now, carefully looking back on my rushing figure. He'd be low to the ground and wishing his way nearer the bird, when suddenly he would coil himself like a cobra and leap into the air at the exact moment the bird flushed, his teeth closing like knives on empty space, so full of another failure to soar he never heard my tattered throat roar whoa! In all fairness to his long-departed spirit (now somewhere, I hope, equipped with wings in some celestial bird field), Ben did catch one quail in flight. He delivered it to me without a scratch as if to say that he was right and I was wrong and that I had a thin outlook on his virtue of perseverance.

I had another setter for a while that was obsessed with a love for automobiles and was equally the most quickly and thoroughly carsick dog I've ever known. I couldn't drive 100 yards until it all came out. But no one ever drove in the driveway and got out of the car before she was in it. And like a lot of setters, she would eat anything this side of a charred stump. I've got to say one thing in her favor, she was fastidious about upchucking. Ordinarily a dog will just throw up, but not Tip. She'd get in the back seat, force her muzzle down in the crack between the cushion and the back of the seat, and then regurgitate.

A five-mile drive to the veterinarian was an adventure that needed at least 24 hours of preparation by fasting. But to give the devil his due, she always outsmarted us by saving something—Lord knows how—and never failed to make a little deposit. Hunting her was next to impossible. I couldn't drive anyplace because she had the areas for miles around the house so scoured out of birds that it was virtually pointless. She wasn't much bigger than a Holstein calf so we just kept her as a house pet. The cat taught her how to catch mice so whenever we heard a scream from a female guest or a muffled grunt of surprise from a male, we knew that Tip was running around the living room with a live mouse hanging by its tail from her mouth. Then with one great swoop of her tongue . . . she'd swallow it!

There are millions of fine-pointing, staunch-holding, turn-and-come-to-the-whistle bird dogs, and the remembered pictures of them standing tall and proud must be wiped from the eyes with a handkerchief. But the dogs that seem to stick even more sweetly in our hearts are the dogs that do it all a bit differently.

We know dogs that ring the doorbell when they want to come in and pull your hand when they want to go out. We know dogs that can count, appreciate dry bourbon Manhattans and sneer obviously when you fluff a crossing shot. If you live on 100 acres of weeded farmland and plant just one expensive rose, we know where the dog will dig his next dusting hole. We know dogs that will not jump up on you in overalls but will bide their time until you're dressed up; dogs that will sleep on the floor of the car unless they're muddy and stinking; and dogs that will not throw themselves through a screen door unless it's new screening. Hunt with him by yourself and he's perfect; brag and hunt him in front of friends and he clowns.

Nobody can fully understand the meaning of love unless he's owned a dog. He can show you more honest affection with a flick of his tail than a man can gather through a lifetime of handshakes. I can't think of anything that brings me closer to tears than when my old dog—completely exhausted after a full and hard day in the field—limps away from her nice spot in front of the fire and comes over to where I'm sitting and puts her head in my lap, a paw over my knee, and closes her eyes and goes back to sleep. I don't know what I've done to deserve that kind of friend, but I'm humble enough not to ask any questions.

I once owned a dog that liked to smile at me and I took a great deal of pleasure in it, as she knew. When you're in the business of being man's best friend you have to develop a broad mind, some individuality and a strong sense of humor. I can't think of anything that would charm me more than someday having a dog that knew how and when to pass a wink my way—dog to Dog Man.

# Chapter 3

# Homebodies

By Tom Hennessey

*FOR AN OLD GEEZER LIKE MYSELF IN HIS MID-EIGHTIES, THE LOSS OF DEAR friends is inevitable. That does not make it any easier, and when Tom Hennessey (1937–2018) passed my heart fell to the ground. A skilled writer and artist, outdoor editor of the* Bangor (Maine) Daily News, *Tom always seemed indestructible to me. He was of the essence of Maine: strong-willed, capable in all weathers, and as Maine as birch bark, rock-rimmed mountains, ruffed grouse, brook trout, black bears, and salty ocean ledges. He was a dog man supreme, never without one, Labrador retrievers and pointing dogs. Tom was a master of capturing powerful emotions in a few words. This piece is one of my favorites, and one of three presented in the pages ahead. They are all excerpted from Tom's book* Feathers 'n Fins *(1989). Here, Tom takes on one of the consistent and major questions in gun dog hunting: Can a dog be excellent in the field and a great companion at home?*

I'd bet that by now someone who caught his first and only salmon three years ago has gone out of his way to inform you that a salmon won't take a fly when the river is shrouded with mist. Don't believe it. I'd also wager that some sage observer who has never been behind a bird dog has made a point of telling you that a woodcock, when flushed, always pauses at the top of its rise. I've always had a sneaking suspicion that this information was passed down by a woodcock. Here's another that could just as well have gone unsaid: You can't keep a hunting dog in the house because it will lose its sense of smell.

I've had the pleasure and privilege of owning a few hunting dogs. Some were kenneled, some took up residence in the house. Without hesitation I can say that my "house dogs" could hunt alongside my "kennel dogs" any day of the week. Misty, a Brittany spaniel who lived in my house and was as good a bird dog as I've seen, would tear the rugs off the floors whenever I put on my hunting hat or picked up a gun. On the same note, Sam and Jake, two birdy characters who occupied my kennel, turned themselves inside out whenever I appeared in hunting togs, or made the mistake of picking up a dog's bell.

Again, I have never been aware of a dog's physical hunting abilities being affected by its abode. If a pup's natural instincts are honed by training and hunting experience, the result is usually a dog stuffed full of desire to hunt. As long as the dog is well cared for, it wouldn't make any difference if it curled up to sleep in a kennel or the Waldorf Towers. Once instilled, that desire is there for the duration.

It is, of course, difficult to have several dogs living in a house. Packs of hounds obviously are kept in kennels. Reference here is to the bird dog, retriever, or, perhaps, the rabbit hound whose owner prefers to make it a part of the family. Those who vacuum the floors and rugs will tell you that a dog in the house creates a lot of work. No question. At present I keep two hunting partners in the house and have to admit that life would often be easier if they were kenneled.

You're probably well aware that a hunting dog who shares your dwelling soon becomes a person disguised as a Brittany spaniel, English setter, beagle, or Labrador retriever. Directly, you'll discover that Duke has established his own schedule, which he must strictly adhere and attend to regardless of your plans or commitments.

Daylight is his signal to stop sleeping. And it won't make any difference if you're plastered into a body cast and have both legs in traction, he'll sit by the bed staring at you and making noises until, mumbling and grumbling, you arise and start the day shift. And try to explain to him, when daylight saving time rolls around, that even though it's light outside, it's only 5 A.M. Doesn't mean a thing. You might as well get up. Sooner war, sooner peace.

A creature of habit, Duke's schedule dictates that he must "turn in" not too long after the supper dishes are dry. Don't, however, think that having a few friends in for the evening will change things. No, siree, bub. No way. Pretty soon you'll notice him pacing and casting you sidelong looks. When that fails, he'll sit in the hallway leading to the bedrooms and run through his repertoire of grunts, groans, whimpers, and whines, which he punctuates with a bark.

Barking. Now there's a subject you would never have become well versed in if ol' Duke were kenneled. There is a bark—"yip"—that, translated, means water. Another—usually a sharp "yap" often preceded by an attention-getting growl—that means food. An indignant "woof" means he wants the scraps on the sideboard, and a high-pitched "yelp" indicates that his ball is under the couch and you'd better get the hell over there and get it out.

The roaring bark that rattles windows, however, he reserves for the paperboy, trash man, UPS driver, Girl Scouts selling cookies, and things that go bump in the night. As you know, that midnight warning can be hazardous to your health. It will hit you straight up out of a sound sleep. Straighten your hair, stop your breathing, and leave you with palpitations of the heart. Not to mention that you'll have to break loose from your wife's headlock.

If you have a live-in Labrador retriever, it's no secret to you that this breed just naturally loves to lug things around. Seldom does a Lab go from one room to another without bringing a "present." Consequently, you spend a lot of time looking for the mates to shoes, boots, socks, slippers, and gloves. Exasperating as it is, it can also become embarrassing.

Take, for instance, the time a few of my hunting pals and I were batting the breeze in my kitchen. Coke, my chocolate Lab, seized the opportunity to visit the laundry room and then sashay onto center stage dragging certain of my wife's unmentionables. Nancy, of course, was present. See what you miss by keeping your dogs kenneled?

A hunting dog that lives in the house learns quickly. Because Jill is in close contact with you she becomes sensitive to the inflections of your voice, your facial expressions, and reads, unerringly, your every change of attitude. Make no mistake about it, she knows your mood and mindset just by the way you pull on your pants. And I'm sure you've noticed that she quietly leaves the room whenever you begin spouting exclamations beginning with "son-of . . ." and ending with names found in the Bible.

I regret that I had to keep some of my dogs in the kennel. For that reason I never got to fully know and understand them. Nor was I able to recognize many of their traits and characteristics. Sure, I had a great rapport with them, especially during hunting season. But other than that, I spent time with them only when I fed them or took them for a run each day. They never got to ride down to the post office or the hardware store, or up to the salmon club to listen to the fireside stories like Coke does. And it bothers me that there must have been nights when, after a day's hunting, my kenneled dogs were sore or lame. Often, I wouldn't become aware of it until the following day.

Can a hunting dog live in the house? You bet. Will ol' feather-finder "lose his nose"? You can't prove it by me. Again, the dogs that have slept curled on my den couch, and who got a portion of my pancakes in the morning, hunted just as hard and performed every bit as well as any dog I had quartered in the kennel. And all of them, insiders and outsiders, lived and hunted into their thirteenth and fourteenth years.

The only drawback of keeping a hunting a dog in the house is that you become ridiculously attached to it. So much, in fact, that you'll feel guilty when you tell your setter or retriever, "Stay!" as you leave the house to go deer hunting. It gets worse, especially if your wife is also addicted to dogs. Nancy has always admonished me for hunting alone. One morning, as Coke and I were getting into my pickup, she leaned out the back door and asked, "Who are you going hunting with?"

"I'm going alone," I answered.

Her pause and reply were as chilling as the pre-dawn darkness: "If something happens to you, how will that dog get home?"

## CHAPTER 4

# A Blue Ridge Hunt

By Christopher Camuto

*THERE IS SO MUCH TO SAY ABOUT CHRIS CAMUTO AND THIS HUNTING DOG STORY that brevity is not possible. The story is excerpted from "Solitary in Winter" in Camuto's book* Hunting from Home: A Year Afield in the Blue Ridge Mountains *(2003). We are afield with Camuto and his dog Patch in a late-season hunt for spooky ruffed grouse. Patch was born of an English pointer father and English setter mother five years before. He wears a bell on his collar to help Camuto keep track of him in the rugged terrain as he goes about his business of probing the cover for ruffed grouse. The prose is evocative and sweeps us along in powerful images that make us part of the story. With apologies to Camuto and his editors, I must admit that the book title,* Hunting from Home, *does not appeal to me. The book is so much more. There are long sections on trout fishing, bird watching, firewood gathering, the changing seasons, and more. The book is a journey through a year in the Blue Ridge at an old farm where nature's changing panorama is always just outside the door. There are also some engaging reflections on the writing process as experienced by Camuto in his Blue Ridge years. Camuto has moved on to teaching at Bucknell University in Pennsylvania and has authored other books on trout, mountain country life, and even wolves.*

In the Blue Ridge, as in Russia, lunch is a rich but small refueling. Today I brought thin slices of deer liver, sautéed this morning in olive oil and garlic, stacked on an onion bagel slathered with grainy Creole mustard. Civilized wild food—the bounty of other hunting, a deer I took at home on the last day of the season. Patch gets some of the liver without the mustard. He never mooches food but is always pleased by the comradeship of sharing a meal. While I chomp through an apple and enjoy clear draughts of cold water, he stares down through the wind-ruffled pines and paces about in the laurel, disappointed that we have put up no birds where he is clearly getting faint whiffs of grouse. But I can tell by how he holds his head that the scent is not on the breeze—we could easily hunt back down through the pines—but traced through the nearby understory where birds have surely been. No tracks betray their recent presence, but I've no doubt a grouse or two is hidden on the precipitous slopes downwind of us—impenetrable escape habitat that gives the game an edge here.

I hitch myself back into the stiff, tin-cloth hunting vest I fancy and cinch it close in front so that I don't catch my shooting elbow in the shoulder strap. I carry a few backcountry essentials in the bird bag and a small bottle of water and some homemade jerky in the left side pocket. The same sharp, bone-handled little pocketknife I use for dressing deer rides in my left pants pocket. I keep powder, wads, shot and other accoutrements in a canvas shoulder bag organized, like a fishing vest, to let me find things by feel. Its weight on my left hip helps balance the heft of the gunstock in my right hand. Halfway through a grouse-hunting day I may look disheveled enough to give a black bear pause for thought, but in my mind's eye I'm as well put together as a banker.

As soon as I stand up from our fifteen-minute break, Patch is all hunt, and I have to whistle him back into coherence. I would not have it any other way. Later, when I'm winded and leg worn, it's Patch's indefatigable energy as much as the lure of grouse that will keep me going. Dogs, like children, set an excellent example, particularly for adventure. And hunting, first and foremost, is adventure—it wasn't just hunger that drew mankind from cave mouth and riverbank. As we set off again up-mountain in the snow, this bird hunting strikes me as gloriously quixotic. It's as if I have equipped myself very practically to bag a Phoenix. As yet unfound and unflushed grouse are, in a sense, mythic—hidden well enough to be as good as unreal until Patch finds them. We are not hunting birds. We are hunting a bird, the next grouse that we flush—a reddish brown beauty digging through the snow for winterberries ten yards or half a mile or a mile from here—and we must find that pound and a half of gallinaceous wildness in this watershed, or the next, or farther on in these lengthy if not endless blue mountains that we love—one bird to find between Georgia and Maine.

With a gloved hand I wipe beaded snowmelt from the well-oiled walnut of the muzzle-loader, a slender straight-stocked gun with a sighting plane that seems to help my cross-dominance and a barrel length suited to my forty-something eyesight. While Patch idles in low, I gently but firmly check the loads with the ramrod, thumb the hammers to half cock, recap the gun and then pull the rabbit ears until I hear another click. For all practical purposes, the flush of a ruffed grouse takes place in the equivalent of what cosmologists call the Planck epoch, the first 10.43 seconds of cosmic history, during which, I am told, there was a lot of high-energy hijinks going on in what astrophysicists call space-time foam, a dense gravitational gumbo out of which the Big Bang boomed and the universe in which Patch and I hunt began to form. It may not advance physics to compare a flushing grouse with the genesis of matter, but the analogy serves to keep us on our toes here in the Blue Ridge. When you are hunting grouse, you are preparing for something like that. If you hunt, as I do, with the nineteenth-century technology of a muzzle-loading shotgun, then you hunt at full cock to have any chance at all.

Friends think I exaggerate about grouse until I take an early-morning hike into spring or summer grouse cover and have to help them ease their hearts back down their throats after a bird bursts loudly from underfoot, disappearing in the confusion before it can be seen (assuming that something unseen can be said to disappear).

"That was a grouse," the explanation always goes.

"You hunt that . . . noise?" the bewildered, admiring query always follows.

Suffice it to say that *Bonasa umbellus* gets into the past tense in a hurry, leaving the air behind it laced with a drift of leaf litter fluttering to the ground like rousted space-time foam.

Just above our lunch spot, we pick up a logging road that slabs along the southeast side of the bulging ridge that will overshadow us for the rest of the afternoon. What is still dry powder in the woods has partially melted and refrozen several times on the road and become the worst kind of snow for walking. The breaking of an inch-thick glaze punctuates every step, burning small quanta of much-needed energy. I resign myself to the additional weight of wet snow clinging to the deep treads of my leather mountain boots. Patch prances around my slogging progress, punching through the crust, the eager staccato of his hunting trot ringing into the quiet air around us, his hunting bell clinking lightly with every move.

For a mile, there's not much cover, but Patch works the unpromising second-growth woods on principle. The relative poverty of the understory—the absence of a natural forest-floor diversity of plant life—is the consequence of overlogging, the logging road itself a mixed blessing I would happily live without. Ruffed grouse, like all forest creatures, require a forest. They do what they can with what woods are left. We, too, take the land as we find it. Despite a century of misuse, the underlying ecology of the Blue Ridge still works to restore and reassert itself.

Each time we crest a curving rise, the winter rush of a stream comes to our ears, a vein of silver in the woods gleaming against a dark seam of mossy bedrock. Above all things, I am a student of the theory and practice of watersheds, the commonplace gatherings of land and water which in the southern Appalachians we call hollows. Our hollows do no less than underwrite the natural life of our mountains. Along with many others, I ask no more than that the natural fullness of our hollows be preserved, not for anyone's pleasure or profit but simply because nature deserves to be. In a culture given over to a monomania of moneymaking and the vulgarity of conspicuous consumption, and those peculiar forms of "development" that lead to impoverishment, preserving nature seems too much to hope for. But you will find in those hollows that survive the rarest, wildest things—black bear, bobcats, rattlesnakes and trout; lady slippers, walking ferns, cushion moss and reindeer lichen; and, among much else, life expressing itself as everything from a scarlet tanager to an ancient eastern hemlock four feet thick. You find in each watershed natural processes reasserting themselves—respiration of oxygen and filtering of water—and the subtle play of soil-building and natural erosion that reshape the mountains moment by moment, eon by eon.

The logging road dead-ends at what I call, with stunning lack of imagination, the big cover, which looks less promising in the glare of a sunny, snow-lined day. Since grouse are skittish on bright days, cloud cover would be welcome. The only thing we have now in our favor is a soft breeze cooing out of the northwest to which Patch pays a good deal of attention. The cover begins at the head of a hollow that broadens out enough to have once supported a mountain farm. It is easiest to visualize this old homestead in winter, when the woods have the clarity of a charcoal drawing and the pathos of its ruins—chimney and hearthstone, logs and window casings, overgrown orchards and sagging hog wire—lie starkly against the rocky, snowbound lay of the land. That one grouse we have hiked and hunted five miles to find is holding in the wild vegetation that has overtaken this old homestead, in the best of times probably a rather poor place but more inviting to my mind's eye than the vanity homes being cantilevered into the mountains in my day, thoughtless gestures of ownership that immediately ruin the stake they claim.

Rutted grouse thrive at these edges where forests reclaim the land from modest human attempts to till and husband. They feed where the land restores itself and take cover, like bear, in its safest, darkest places. I take each bird we flush to be a sudden reification of an indigenous wildness I love like bedrock and flowing water. Ruffed grouse are not a symbol of anything. They are the thing itself—wild life flying up in the face of human attempts to use nature. But what holds the grouse in this watershed is not the clear-cuts the U.S. Forest Service claims as a form of game management, but a swath of old growth a half mile from here that nurtures the birds through most of the year. Given a choice between a housing development and a ten-year-old clear-cut, you will find the grouse in the recovering clear-cut. But what they really prefer—what they preferred for the millions of years before the Forest Service, with the encouragement of the well-heeled gentlemen of the Ruffed Grouse Society, started managing the hell out of them—is a true forest at their back. For grouse, as well as for those who love the woods, edge habitat without an undisturbed forest behind it is an ecological fraud. But these old mountain home sites are more like natural forest openings than the slash-choked, road-scarred clear-cuts taxpayers have been duped into subsidizing for fifty years.

Before we get too close to that promising old dwelling place tangled in grapevine and greenbrier, I bring Patch to heel. I take ten minutes to fully catch my breath during which, for Patch's benefit, I pretend to tend the gun. This face-saving is pointless. He has been stopping to wait for me to catch up with him ever since we left the truck. When I'm ready, we work our way together through the wooded open slope downwind of an overgrown meadow that has become a deer yard, to judge from the game trails and neat piles of oval scat I always find there. That northwesterly breeze combs through the heart of this good cover right to us.

Just below the meadow I release Patch with his favorite words—"Hunt 'em up"—but whispered, so that he knows I want him working close.

With habitat as good as overgrown old fields and a senescent orchard bordered by coralberry, grape, greenbrier and laurel, it's best to assume game is at hand. Beyond the house site at the meadow, small farm fields regrown in locust, red maple, sumac and yellow birch stretch between the two cold, thin creeks that drain this odd, anvil-flat hollow. At the head of the hollow, ranks of chestnut oak and northern red oak occupy the long ridge to the west and throw sharp shadows on the snow. Hemlock and white oak have settled the rich ground below us, although the heartening diversity of tree species here belies a broad descriptive summary. I'd guess there are a dozen different kinds of trees in any hundred-foot square. Those rocky, twisting creeks are tied together with rusted barbed wire that sags wherever its hand-hewn locust posts have rotted away. What's left of that summer labor now supports tunnels of the dense, wild braid of vegetation where birds and small mammals thrive.

As we approach, this choice cover, I'm birdier than Patch, which is disappointing. I may think, already composing a story in my head, that a grouse will flush from the squat ruins of the chimney or burst from the snow beneath an attractive gathering of laurel, but ruffed grouse don't comply with my picturesque fantasies. If Patch doesn't smell them, the birds are not there, or they are there but he has not yet caught the curling scent plume that will dampen that wagging tail and slow his steps until he locks up on point. Besides, as I say, in winter we are not hunting birds, but a bird, a solitary winter grouse on the side of a mountain, something very tiny in a landscape in which we ourselves are small. Watching Patch, hoping his generalized interest will screw itself down to endgame attentiveness, I stop trying to guess where that bird might be because it will not, on principle, be where I expect it. That much I know. Which is to say I know nothing.

Assorted wrens and warblers flush like sparks as Patch works the cover, carving a trough through the snow, a wild Rorschach of his efforts. In the presence of game scent, he pays the songbirds no mind. He may be a mixed breed, but he has inherited good gifts from his parents and is a more robust dog than either of them. He will sleep deeply tonight, but in the field he is tireless. He hunts until I need a break, but he never initiates one on his own. *I hunt, therefore I am*, his driving joy and butt-wagging energy seem to say. And now that he has outgrown his adolescent penchant for chasing rabbits and deer—for miles and hours—he is as good a bird-finding companion as you could want.

I like to think that the two of us look good hunting that old home site in winter—Patch studying along the downwind edge of a thicket, me at port arms ready for a wild flush, the snow-eased landscape lying indifferently about us, flat winter light making everything one. We look good hunting, I like to think. It seems fair and balanced—the man, the dog, the grouse that is or isn't there, the invisible but palpable breeze that leads us on. The miles we have walked. The scene is balanced, too, between pleasure and fatigue, between wanting to stop and wanting to go on, between satisfaction with what is and desire for more—for the clinking of the dog's bell to stop suddenly as Patch freezes delicately on point, his right forepaw raised in that dainty gesture of self-restraint by means of which he relinquishes the end of the hunt to me. And then for a bird to flush forever in front of us. You get to thinking like a mountain in the mountains. You get to wanting to be as strong and graceful as the wild land and wild life around you.

Once we get in the thick of things, that cooing breeze swirls about us unpredictably, eddying along the edges of the big timber that surrounds this enclave, and so we work the forty acres in a series of ellipses and epicycles that would have given Ptolemy pause for thought. A high wind with weather in it roars faintly overhead, but we are in the lee of the main ridge and won't have to worry about what is coming from the west until we cross that saddle going back on the logging road. Patch is clearly culling through old scent for something fresh, but we haven't seen bird tracks all day. Deer, fox, plenty of rabbit, and turkey on the logging road, but no short, thick arrow of grouse print—an unmistakable sign—to lead us on. But the birds may be roosting nearby and flying into the cover to feed. Who knows?

Unlike deer, grouse are difficult to observe. Even a dedicated grouse hunter has very little contact with them throughout the year. As I have said, they usually introduce themselves by leading. And books on grouse are an absurd mess of contradictions, half-truths and folklore. The experts tell us to hunt them where their food is, which is to tell us everything and nothing. One study in New York State discovered that ruffed grouse eat a thousand things (994, to be precise), which is to discover that they can feed anywhere they like in a healthy forest. They are, like all wild animals, proof of the health of a forest, a revelation, when you do find them, of at least a thousand things.

We work the irregular meadow edge thoroughly, expecting that any moment a bird will flush back into the woods and start a chase. We are at our best now, dicing the cover up with our combined attention. Patch effortlessly cuts here and there, his hunting bell chanting short musical phrases as he stops and starts, body curved and shoulders hunched in an intense questioning of all the scents filtering through his conscious-ness. I'm conscious that we are up in the mountains with the watershed to ourselves—I haven't heard a shot all day—hunting the snowbound woods as if it were our job. My legs have recovered from the burn of the snow-dragging hike. My heart and lungs feel strong. The gun is light in my hands. I follow Patch, trying as best I can to anticipate where his interest may lead. But no grouse flushes from the meadow edge.

Patch slakes his thirst in the snow-cold creek that flows along the far edge of the old field. The brilliant water recharges him. He bounds downstream through the snow until an overgrown fence line turns his head. He works it carefully, studying it in places, circling possibilities, not wanting to miss anything but not wanting to be misled. He is poised, as a good bird dog should be, between eagerness and diligence. Once you get on good cover, your concentration gathers around the immediacy of this intent hunting. The horizon of your attention shrinks to the ground between you and the dog and the cover just beyond him. This hunting is what you hunt for.

The fence line takes us across the slope toward the second stream a half mile away. Before we are halfway through our first pass, a grouse flushes forty yards downwind of us—a gray blur driven by a muffled whir heading downslope. Patch had neither scented nor bumped the bird. Judging from the way he is riveted to the fence line, it must have been running well in front of us, which grouse often do. In fact, I find its pudgy track winding along the fence line a little farther on. A hand signal and my own changed direction get Patch going where the bird now leads us. When he gets down to where the gray blur did its touch-and-go, he looks over his shoulder, seeming to acknowledge that I may have some usefulness on these maneuvers.

Now we need to get down to business. As a puppy, Patch would have chased the bird to oblivion. During his career as a two-year-old flushing pointer, he would have kept bumping it just out of gun range all the way to Pennsylvania. Now he gathers himself like Valery's elder dog and tries to carefully close the distance between himself and the bird, checking to make sure I am still with him, following behind and to one side. Patch is not just a good nose; he has experience in the ways of grouse and remembers every move they have made. We share the same memories of failed and successful hunts. But his awareness of the great birds we have pursued is fine-grained, detailed, subtle and complex. My only knowledge of them is the flush and two or three seconds of escape flight, if I see them at all. We are both more grousy than we used to be, sadder and wiser and a little harder to fool.

But despite Patch's best efforts, the bird gets up out of range again on its own, farther out than before—another gray blur tracing the contour of the slope down and away. The confidence of its curving, ground-hugging glide, and the fact that it is still downwind of us, suggests that this is not our bird today, but a decoy sent by the gods to exercise our judgment or our legs. When a grouse, a rich reddish brown bird, is far enough away to turn gray, it is as good as gone as any deer flashing a fat white tail at you. Still, we have unlocked our prey from a silent winter mountainside—effected the metamorphosis we came to see—and need to follow up. We have two hours of light, and I know this terrain well. We will suspend judgment and exercise our legs.

I whistle Patch to circle broadly with me back toward the first creek we crossed. No point in pressuring a skittish bird downslope. We follow that creek downstream, hoping to put at least a quartering breeze between the grouse and ourselves, which should give Patch a better chance to close in and pin it. As we hurry along, the snowbound woods look different, full of our expectation now that we've made game. The landscape glows and pulses. But except for the thin creek dashing through a gauntlet of snow and icy rock, nothing moves in the woods with us. By the look of the open timber, recovering second-growth oak and hickory, I'd guess that rousted bird is headed for distant cover.

We slip downstream a mile or so with as little fanfare as possible, but that breeze never turns Patch's head. I call a halt just above the confluence of the creek we've been following with the second, larger stream that drains the hollow. We're at the point of another triangle. Together, the two streams have dug a deep, oval pool where, hunting here in October, I've watched brook trout spawn in shafts of golden autumn light. Today, the trout are tucked away, suspended in the cold, very near the essence of winter's interior stillness. The empty pool, like the empty woods, seems full. The trout and the grouse, whose presence we feel keenly in their absence, are secret sharers of the ongoing life of this watershed of which we catch only glimpses.

If the bird is above us, we'll find it on the way back up, following the second stream. But I suspect that wary grouse is far below us in thick cover along the river these tributaries feed, cover we've hunted hard and well earlier in the season when the birds were still bunched up and offered easier shooting. As I've said, we cannot hunt it all at once. For safety's sake, I want to be back where the logging road dead-ends at the home site before daylight disintegrates into darkness. In winter, dusk won't hold a working light for you the way it does in other seasons. The finest trout you ever catch will rise in the forgiving dusk of late spring or in the nearly endless, sometimes starlit dusk of summer. But daylight vanishes suddenly, like a grouse or a trout, in midwinter, and it's dangerous to be picking your way through these cliff-pocked woods in the dark.

Our futile pursuit had taken us out of the best of the big cover, but we get back into it working uphill. We have the wind fully in our favor again—too much wind, really. Gusty blusters of unfriendly cold hammer at us, and Patch gets giddy with an overload of information in his nose, impertinent data on every grouse from here to West Virginia. We pull ourselves together just below all that good cover. Good cover *looks* good, birds or no. I stop to get a hooded pullover on, a windproof fleece I need in this punching cold. I put a fingerless glove on my left hand but leave my right hand bare. When we get up on those relatively flat oldfields, my heart and lungs slow down and I feel enough energy and focus left in me to take a bird.

When we get back to the lower fence line, I cut Patch loose again. He busts through some nasty brier-choked shrub and rotting slash and then gets up in the laurel above me. When the loose, running jangle of his hunting bell shifts to toll the quick feints and tight turns of his making game, that artful decision making—*not here, not here, this way, this way, not here, this way, this way, here*—I'm all ears. And when the bell tightens down, somehow quick and slow all at once—*this way, this way, this way, here*—I listen hardest to the silence of his taut point. *Here. Ahead. Here. Right here. Right here. Now.*

Halfway through the nanosecond it takes for this final message to spark from dog to man, the grouse gets up, through no fault of Patch's. I'm twenty yards from the point and the flush, but this one I see coming. I shoulder the gun and paint through the bird, letting my hips and shoulders turn my head, which is nestled to the stock. When my lead is right, the bird seems to have stopped moving and I no longer hear the distracting sound of its flight. I'm conscious only of a window of space-time in front of it, which my concentration enlarges, and that there is no light left in the background. This grouse is flying into night, which is waiting in the woods all around us. This day, this hunt, is almost over.

When you hunt well, you shoot well. Deep into the country, the country gets deep into you. A day over rough terrain has steadied me for this moment. Sometimes, as Turgenev wrote, the bird flies smoothly into your shot string. I picked the crumpled grouse up from bloodless snow at the base of a sugar maple, where Patch had come, too tired for the war dance, to look at it. The dog, the bird, the man—the mountainside, the sugar maple, the sudden dark—we are all in this together.

I'm too tired, mentally and physically, to fully appreciate the bird. There will be time for that later. I brush the snow from it and briefly look it over, finding beads of blood on its breast. I spread its wings and tail out for Patch to see and smell. *Bird. Good dog. Bird. Bird.* His grave eyes gleam.

In ten minutes, we are back on the logging road, a good hour from the truck. The glazed snow glows in the dark, curving down the mountain. The woods are familiar and strange, silent inside of the hollow sound of a full-blown westerly that arrived with nightfall, silent against the crunch of my footsteps and the musical rattle of Patch's bell. I listen for owls but hear no owls tonight. In places, I smell deer. The universe expands above us at forty or sixty or seventy kilometers per second per megaparsec, but we are too weary and content to think about larger things. Orion hunts overhead with two dogs in tow, like Valery with Touman and Chara. I trust my Russian friends are well. Patch and I are satisfied with this long day. We've worn ourselves out pretty well on these old mountains and, when we get far enough down the road to encounter our own tracks, we each take advantage of the trail we broke coming up, carefully measuring out the energy we have saved for going home.

## CHAPTER 5

# The Old Maid

By Havilah Babcock

*THE SOUTH CAROLINA LOWCOUNTRY WAS HOME TO HAVILAH BABCOCK (1898–1964), and he wrote about that region with the prose skills of a natural storyteller. An English professor by trade, he turned his creative powers to such homegrown subjects as catalpa worm fishing, largemouth bass, and his favorite—bobwhite quail hunting. His anthologies featured a diverse lineup of tales, but quail hunting was always the main subject, as in* Tales of Quails 'n Such *(1985), where this story appeared, and in other tomes, including* My Health Is Better in November *and* I Don't Want to Shoot an Elephant.

Good covey dogs are, as Lincoln said of Civil War generals, "as plenty as blackberries." Hardy, spirited rangers that will put up whatever there is to be put up and give you your money's worth day in and out. That is, in good bird country.

But if you are ever fortunate enough to get your hands on a real single-bird dog, don't forget to say your prayers regularly. It's the only thing I'd steal without the slightest compunction of conscience—a really good one.

For a covey dog, give me a pointer—stamina, dash, derring-do. For a singles dog, give me a setter—patience, thoroughness, precision. Just one man's experience, and if it doesn't jibe with yours don't sue me for it. All you could get would be good covey dogs, anyway. Single-bird dog is in my wife's name.

Also, if you care to, you can give me a setter that has been spayed. And I'll take my setter with a little age on her. Rare old Ben Franklin advised a young man to pick an old woman to have his affairs with. The same consideration underlies my nomination of an oldish lady for singles hunting.

Funny thing, too, I never saw a good singles dog with a fancy name. A friend of mine has a sedate and aging setter whose name is Bess, but whom we always refer to as the Old Maid, which just suits her mincing delicacy and fastidious thoroughness in the field. The Old Maid is not in the canine Who's Who. She has never been in a field trial, nor had her picture in the papers. And you never heard of her. But I know a couple of hard-headed hunters who wouldn't trade her for a first cousin of the Grand Champion, once removed. Will Carrington is the other fellow. In fact, the Old Maid really belongs to Will, although he always refers to her as "ours." I have mainly a borrowing interest in her. In golf, you drive for fun and putt for money. In bird shooting, you hunt coveys for excitement and singles for your game. This is truer now more than ever before.

Time was when birds were so plentiful that covey hunting would give a man all that he wanted, and more than he was decently entitled to. I reckon such a time once was. If not, the old-timers I've listened to are a raft of unhallowed prevaricators.

I know a whimsical old gentleman who is fond of saying: "I ain't the man I used to be. Never was." Maybe it's the same with birds.

Time was when Bob was a self-contained and chancy fellow who held his ground until properly flushed. But he is not so stable as of old. He has become a bit jumpy here of late, often flushing at the least provocation. In fact, latter-day Bob is becoming an ungentlemanly trickster, full of sly ruses and pettfoggin' ways. Or to put it kindlier, Bob has developed a bad case of the D.T.'s. And pray who wouldn't have, what with the "reclamation" of his refuges by a benevolent and misguided government, the encroachments of a more scientific agriculture, and a highly mobilized Coxey's army a-gunning for him day in and day out?

For good and sufficient reasons, then, the singles dog is coming into his own. And sometimes local weather conditions join other factors to make such a specialist a prime necessity.

For instance, in Lowcountry South Carolina, where I pay a few taxes and shoot a lot of birds, the 1939 hunting season opened in the middle of a drought. There had been no rainfall for more than two months. Fields, woods, even the devilish bays were as dry as tinder. Leaves rattled ominously whenever you stepped. There had been no rain to dissolve the dust from the undergrowth, and our dogs were forever sneezing and coughing. Trailing conditions were next to impossible. As the season advanced, the drought became more pronounced, and the birds more jittery and unstable.

Of the 38 coveys that Will and I raised during the first week, 27 flushed prematurely, slithering away at the first approach of the dogs and holing up in the impenetrable bays, where a few bird hunters and no gentleman will follow. Singles hunting proved equally disastrous. The dogs would either run over the ground-hugging singles in the dusty straw or flush them in the powder-dry, clattering leaves. It was not the fault of the dogs. Good hunters they were—Jackie, Pedro and High Pocket. Just too fast for dry-weather hunting.

During that unhappy first week, Will and I had one experience that will warm the cockles of any bird hunter's heart, however old and hardened a sinner that he might be. A whopping big covey roared up from a pea patch ahead of us and sailed away to a field of golden broom straw. They didn't clump down in a body but deployed nicely in twos and threes. As perfect a layout for singles shooting as a body could wish.

"That's the sort of thing that keeps a fellow huntin'," Will grinned. "The sort of thing that don't happen too often in this here modern society."

"Sure looks like the payoff," I agreed. "And the answer to the bird supper that we've invited all those people to."

"Yes, sir," seconded Will as we strode confidently toward the field. "If a fellow can't fill his pockets with such a layout as that, he'd better quit." But our hopes were short-lived. While we were still a hundred yards away, birds began to pop out of the dry straw and head for the distant and forbidding bay. We started to shout at the dogs and run—which a good hunter seldom does much of. But to no purpose.

Sweeping through the straw, our dogs routed those singles one by one. Even respectable dogs will sometimes lose their heads when things are popping too fast. When we got there, not a blessed bird was left. What can take an unruffled and philosophical spirit and tear it to tatters like that?

"And that's what makes a fellow quit huntin', I reckon." Will slumped forlornly on a log. "Twenty birds in that covey, and we got how many? Nary a one!"

"Pretty thorough job they made of it," I added dismally. "We hunted for that chance a whole week, and had it ruined in two minutes."

"Straw too dry."

"Dogs too fast."

"Birds nervous."

Thus we tersely diagnosed the case, and Will added the clincher: "Ain't goin' to be any better until it rains, and . . ."—he looked toward the discouraged skies—"it ain't gonna rain no more."

"We got to do something about it," I ultimatumed.

"Yeh. Got to," Will dully agreed. "What you got in mind?"

"Nothing."

I chewed a sassafras twig and wondered if I could put a notion in Will's head without his suspecting my authorship.

"By the way," I said, trying hard to sound honest, "how old is the Old Maid?"

"She's pushin' eleven."

"Too old to hunt, of course."

"Yeh. Too old."

"Fattish, too, I reckon."

"Yeh. Fattish, too."

"We agreed last year not to hunt her any more, besides."

"Sure. Shook hands on it and promised Mary."

"Never do to lie to Mary."

A pretty satisfactory conference, I figured, knowing Will as I do. And when we met the next morning, there was the Old Maid in person, an amiable old blue-ticked Llewellin, squatting like a fat dowager on the front seat of the car. And there was Will, looking happy and sort of sheepish.

"Got her but had to stand a lot of kidding from Mary. Said we ought to be ashamed of falling back on an old pensioner, us with our two-hundred-dollar dogs. But my pride is gettin' easy to swallow here lately."

"Of course, we've got to favor her," I conceded, fondling a shaggy ear.

It was soon apparent that the Old Maid would do her own favoring. Quietly she trotted behind us, contenting herself with an occasional excursion to check up on a likely thicket or a tentative clue that the other dogs had found and abandoned. Nothing could induce her to try her fortunes with the rollicking trio that swept the fields ahead. The Old Maid knew why she had been brought along, and she knew her own limitations, which is about the finest thing either dog or man can learn.

Within half an hour the other dogs had raised a fine covey, the birds flushing wild as usual and sailing off into an overgrown field.

"Now let's call those rambunctious hellions in, tie them to a sapling, and let the Old Maid speak her piece," decided Will.

So saying, he produced three lengths of rope and tied up the traveling trio, much to their disgust and the jeopardy of the sapling.

The Old Maid had seen the covey and watched it down. As we approached, she trotted sedately ahead of us and began to insinuate herself through the undergrowth. Step by step she minced along, sneaking through the dry weeds and straw like a ghost. "Walking on pins and needles," Will called it. And presently she announced a single, which Will brought down, and which she retrieved with the same daintiness, carefully retracing her steps on the retrieve to prevent invading untested ground.

"Notice how she came out the same way she went in? Old thing doesn't mean to risk a flush," beamed Will.

"I don't need a guidebook to the Old Maid's virtues, thank you," I answered, and bagged the next bird myself.

Back she went unbidden to her task, tiptoeing tediously about, warily testing every clump of weeds for her high-strung quarry. Once she pointed a single with a bird in her mouth—a heartwarming sight however often you have ever seen it. And once she brought in a twosome—not to be dramatic, but because common sense dictated such a procedure when two birds lay side by side.

When her tedious job was done, bless my soul if the Old Maid hadn't pointed and retrieved nine of those singles without a mishap or accidental flush!

One of her traits that had particularly struck me was her quiet self-sufficiency. Not once had she let her anxiety to retrieve betray her into rashness, as might well have happened with a less practiced hand. Not once did she require instructions as to her job. We never talk much when the Old Maid is on a hard case. Matter of fact, she never thinks such a touchy situation appropriate for idle chatter. When a bird was downed, Will simply announced the fact. In him she had complete faith, never requiring reassurance and never relaxing her quest.

That very thoroughness of hers cost us an hour's delay the next day and gave me a sidelight on Will's training methods. Will has a way of his own with the dogs, and the incident, although a trifle irritating at the time, was highly revealing.

A wing-tipped bird had scurried into a hollow log and baffled the Old Maid's efforts to extricate it. Valiantly she laid siege to that log, prying, scratching and jamming her muzzle into the hollow, but to no avail. Nor did our added efforts help any. I tried to talk her into resigning the case, but no amount of persuasion could induce her to abandon the beleaguered quarry.

"We can't do anything with that derned dog, Will. We've lost fifteen minutes already. Tell her to be reasonable and come on."

"Just against her principles to leave a wounded bird, I reckon," replied Will.

"Heck! Pitch another one near the log and let her retrieve that. Maybe that'll satisfy the fussy old dame."

"That would hardly be honest, would it?" demurred Will. "A dog should be taught not to lie. Best way to teach 'em that is not to lie to them. I taught her the same thoroughness when she was a puppy, and I'm not goin' to fuss with her now. She's right and we're wrong, only she has more time than we have."

With that, Will smiled indulgently and stalked off across the field. A quarter of an hour later he was back with an ax and a wedge, and we fell to splitting that hollow log so that the Old Maid could satisfy her conscience.

"That's what comes of having too good a dog," I chided peevishly. "And damned if you ain't as stubborn as she is."

But in my heart I felt a sneaking admiration for the pair of them.

For the next four weeks, as long as the dry weather lasted, we followed the same procedure: letting the other dogs hunt the coveys and the Old Maid the singles, especially when conditions called for delicate maneuvering. They were altogether the most satisfying hunts I've ever had. And three-fourths of the birds we bagged during that time we owed to the patience and finesse of the old lady.

"That dame is a genius, and nothing else," I conceded after a particularly fine day. "Just as an academic question, Will: what will you take for your half of her?"

"Well there's my car, my gun and the other dogs. There's the farm, the mules and the kitchen stove. And there's my wife, maybe. But the Old Maid, I reckon she's about the only thing on the place that ain't for sale."

"Think I'll put her in a story," I ventured.

"If you do, be sure to say she ain't for sale."

"No dogs like her nowadays, Will," I insisted, caressing a ragged ear. "Sometimes I think that nothing is as good as it used to be, anyway."

"Oh, you're getting mellow over your shootin' these last few days. Matter of fact, the puppy I'm workin' on now will be just as good as the old lady in time. It's not hard, if a fellow has the patience, time, the birds—and a dog to start with. But unless a man is cut out by Providence to fool with dogs, I reckon he'd better hire his trainin' done. Best money he ever spent. Or buy one already trained. If he's an important fellow that gets off just now and then, he'd better buy a dog that's set in his ways, an old dog that's got more sense than he has—one he can't ruin. And I don't mean any harm by that. A fellow has got to be out of a job and not worried about it to train a dog right, I reckon."

## CHAPTER 6

# The Family Honor

By Nash Buckingham

*Someone once wrote, "The best long-range duck and goose load is a good retriever." Nash Buckingham (1880–1971), a legend in hunting literature, shows us the truth of that statement in this story from his first book,* De Shootinest Gent'man and Other Tales *(1934). "Mr. Nash," as many called him, hunted and wrote in the halcyon years of all waterfowl and shotgun hunting, from the late 1800s into the early 1900s. His experience, particularly in waterfowl hunting, was immense. Here his attention is focused on a Chesapeake Bay retriever. Not as popular as the Labrador retriever, the "Chessie" was and still is a powerful dog, a breed strong-willed and thought by many to be more difficult to train and handle than the friendly Labs. Mr. Nash will tell you all about one of his favorites. (Editor's Note: In the Old South of Buckingham's day, the expression "Marse" for "Master" was sometimes used instead of "Mister" as a manner of respect. This story has been edited from the original version.)*

Pat, for short of the stud book's pompous tally, was one from a litter of six Chesapeake Bay puppies whelped of noble sire and dauntless dam. Bred in the purple and fearless, intelligent water dogs, Pat's old folks, Count and Beck, dared conditions that any day could produce to balk their line of business duty. Acknowledged king and queen of their respective territories; he on his side of the Potomac—she on hers. Duck gunners had long since been wont to seek hungrily and bid high for their progeny. More than once, after some particularly brilliant retrieve, old Beck had heard Marse Henry offered all kinds of real money for her. But Beck had quit worrying. When such "cracks" were pulled, Marse Henry's eyes twinkled as he knocked the ashes out of his pipe, just to prolong the suspense of negotiation. Clearing his throat by way of possibly appearing even more interested, he'd drawl: "Have you got as much as five hundred bucks to lay on the barrel head for a sure enough Chesapeake?" "Yep," more than one wildfowler had shot back at him, "I've got all of that for the like of her!" "Fine," Marse Henry would assent, restuffing his smoke-screener. "In that case you jus' keep on savin' up an' when you've got a thousand or so to go on top of that five hundred—why—why— even then I doubt if it would do any good to take another wallop at me. Why, hell's bells! Five grand or a stack of greenbacks high as the Washington monument for this old sister wouldn't interest me in the least." And knowing Henry, they knew he meant just that, foolish and sentimental as it seemed or sounded.

But Marse Henry, good friend and neighbor that he is, rarely, if ever, sold a pup. He made a present here and there until, out of Beck's last presentation, only little sister Pat and big brother Fritz remained. Doc had had first pick, but I'm coming to that later. Somehow, first one and then another of her babies "turned up missing." Drifted away mysteriously while Beck was out foraging. Those last two, Fritz and Pat, grew increasingly precious. What a mother! How she petted and loved and licked them. And with what ominous ferocity she guarded them, too! A grand specimen of the breed, old Beck. A great sway-backed, wavy-withered, lemon-eyed creature; massively compact and rugged. Lying there amid sun patches filtering through Marse Henry's apple orchard, she tenderly dreamed away her youngsters' puppyhood. Hard to tell apart, those two brown, furry balls; rolling, leaping and snarling in rough dispute for possession of the long-suffering house kitten. Beck's misty, blinky eyes wandered from her darlings—along the Maryland heights and far across the lordly Potomac toward Virginia and Mount Vernon. What were her thoughts? Your guess is as good as mine. Of canvasbacks, blackheads, or whistlers slithering into Marse Henry's decoys? Or that terrible day she broke through sharp skim-ice offshore and was trapped in a floe? She had cut her forelegs to ribbons crashing shoreward for her life. A close call, that! But she had delivered the goods, a mere "trash duck," at that. No, Beck and death weren't entire strangers. But stuff like that was all water gone under the bridge—all in her day's work. When their times came, she didn't want Pat or Fritz "showing yellow," either. Anything but that. Happy all her days long, Beck. No dog on earth could ever have had as kindly a master, or a happier home. Dog heaven, that farm! All and more than one wanted to eat—and such grub! Marse Henry to hunt crows with and pitch driftwood for her and the babies to retrieve. And plenty of rabbits to jump and chase through the corn and pasture. If all that was in Beck's mind, she had a great deal to be thankful for, for she gave value received and a golden disposition. Maybe, just about then, she was thinking of how Fritz and Pat happened into this jolly old duck-shooting world.

Last New Year's Day—of all times! For quite a while Beck and the farmhold had been looking forward to a "blessed canine event." Marse Henry had been overly solicitous of her lately. Beck had noticed him looking at her, counting on his fingers. On several occasions he had quietly latched the kennel and slipped off down to the blind without her. And maybe she hadn't howled. The Colonel had to come and tell her to hush, and ask if she wasn't ashamed of herself making all that fuss. Then he'd grinned and given her a piece of sweet corn-pone. Good old girl!

That particular New Year's morning had fetched in a keen, northwest blow, a regular rip-snorter that had been brewing all night. Beck heard it moaning and then roaring around the snug dog house. She knew there'd be drift ice in the river, and a nasty chop for any dog to buck. When Marse Henry and Doc stalked through the yard snapping their flashlights and adjusting packs, Beck tumbled out, flourished about and made it plain that she expected to punch the clock as a matter of course. But Marse Henry said, "No, no, old folks, not today—the hay for yours. 'Doc' prescribes rest and quiet!" Then he collared her and patted and joked her back into the shed; thinking, too, he'd snapped down the door-catch on his way out. But duck hunters have a way of hurrying, with daylight in the offing. After a bit, when howling hadn't prevailed and restlessness wouldn't slack, Beck suddenly shoved hard against the door—and it swung open. The outer gate was a tight squeeze, but she made it. It was easy, then, to track her men down the river road. She caught up just as they deposited their plunder outside the shack. That was Beck's first "break."

"Well, I'll jus' be—looka' here, 'Doc,'" Marse Henry cussed, trying to frown at her as she waddled up to them; "if here ain't old Beck—why— why—I locked that door—how th'—, you gotta' go home—this ain't any way to run a duck hunt—you ain't got any business foolin' roun' this river a day like today." Beck sensed this meant business. Marse Henry was sputtering sore. The situation called for a number of tail wags to get in close enough to roll over and do a "beg." "Heck of a note," cluttered Marse Henry, only he didn't say "heck." "It'll take half an hour to lead her back up yonder—darn near daylight—and we can't tie her here on this cold bank." Then Doc made a suggestion, and old Beck got her second "break." "Henry," said Doc, "I'll tell you what—let's take her on out to the blind—it's warm and comfortable and she can lie there just as safely as she would in the kennel—anyway—there's a day left—isn't there?" It was coming light with a rush, and Marse Henry weakened. He had bent to rub Beck behind her ears, so she snuggled up closer and gave him a pays-poke. That settled it. "Well," agreed Marse Henry, "all right, but she mustn't do a lick of work!" The blind, that winter, was staked fifty yards offshore. Ira, the handyman, was just skiffing in from anchoring the decoys. A hundred or more black, bobbing specks were swinging with the tide. With much ado as to Beck's comfort, all hands loaded in and Ira effected an easy transfer. Marse Henry lit an oil stove in one end of the hooded blind, and made Beck curl up in some warm straw and sacks at the other end. Ira paddled ashore while Marse Henry and Doc shoved shells into their heavy double guns and made ready to operate on any early arrivals. Marse Henry, suddenly remembering something, had just picked up a chain and turned toward Beck's end when Doc hissed, "Henry—Henry —mark left—down—quick." Marse Henry ducked, and grabbed for his gun. There was a second or two's quivering ecstasy that is prelude to man's symphony of sport—then—pop—pop—poppity—pop! A drain rattled on the floor! After all, it was instinct and business pride, with Beck. The family honor must be upheld. She just had to go, and that was all there was to it. Up in a flash; a headlong plunge past Marse Henry's rubber-booted shins—and a leaping dive off the outside splash step. Sheer, teeth-gritting nerve carrying her and a precious burden through an icy surge. More than she had bargained for, at that. She realized it, pretty quick, too. But, somewhere out there—somewhere out there—puff-puff—cripples might be getting away. That was her business, cripples and dead 'uns. Things would just have to take care of themselves—she'd see them through. She had heard but lost Marse Henry's swearing and bawling—"Come back he'ah, you ole fool." But just then she'd topped a swell, sighted a still struggling canvasback, and flung herself toward it through crest smother. Three such trips she plowed, at each return successfully eluding Marse Henry's frantic efforts to snatch her collar and haul her into the hide. Really, she was about "all in," and glad to climb in with the last victim. She was panting heavily and had a draggy feeling.

Never had she seen or heard Marse Henry take on so; swearing to himself and wishing to this, that and the other he had herded her back to the kennel in the first place. Half the time she couldn't tell whether he was cussin' or cryin'! He and Doc made all manner of palaver over her after she slunk into the straw. Doc dried her off with an old piece of quilt, and Marse Henry moved the heater closer. She remembered dropping into a doze. Up on the shooter's bench something was said about "the greatest exhibition of instinct!" Doc was doing most of the talking. Marse Henry was still cussing himself. Shortly thereafter, at any rate during a later bombardment, Marse Henry and Doc, in the act of a hurried reload, caught two or three faint whimpers from old Beck's corner and some scuffling about in the hay. Having, at one time or another, become familiar with such sounds, they gazed at each other in amazed incredulity. Then Doc dove for a hurried preliminary examination. And Doc knows his dogs, too. "Get busy, Doc, this is your first case of the year," grinned Henry, standing around first on one foot and then the other, while cans and blackheads whisked by unheeded. Doc announced, after awhile, that mother and children were doing as well as could be expected. Meanwhile Ira had brought the boat, and Marse Henry sent him to the house for a flannel-lined basket and the car. The shoot went A.W.O.L. for awhile and there was reunion and celebration at the house. Marse Henry chuckled as he and Doc lugged their afternoon's bag up the road at nightfall. "Those sure ought to be great dogs—born right there in the duck blind—what do you know about that—if they haven't got everything a water-dog needs, then there's no such thing as prenatal influence." To which Doc made answer, taking cover with small loss of professional dignity, "Not all of us agree, Henry, that there is any such thing—however—I—er—ahem—am—er—inclined to believe—er—that—er—this particular case may prove a light-shedding and strengthening factor in affirmative observation!" "Well," came back Marse Henry, "all that you're talking about may be so, but be that as it may, in view of medical services rendered, your general all-around participation and the happy termination of this salubrious occasion, you get first litter pick—that's fair, ain't it?" And maybe Doc didn't grab while the choosing was good and old Beck in a consenting frame of friendship.

Well, perhaps some such memories flitted through her mind as she lay under the apple trees that afternoon, watching Patsy and Fritz devil the kitty.

Autumn was in the very air. Hillsides flamed and russet girdles wove in and out among coniferous headlands. Came cool days when Marse Henry, meeting me on the street, cocked an eye aloft and allowed: "Boy, there's that old feelin' in th' vicinity o' my mind sorter like ducks—how 'bout you?" I'd admit it, and find myself unconsciously but hopefully following Marse Henry's slant skyward for a chance glimpse of early migrants. You never can tell about ducks. Then we'd talk ducks awhile longer and branch off onto guns and loads. That particular day, however, Marse Henry had said, "I guess you'll be headin' south, yourself, before long—mos' any day now?" He opened the old pipe's throttle, a sure sign of some truly deep stuff! "How'd you like to take Pat down south where ducks and geese are so plentiful—and—and—sorter start breakin' her for me?"

There is the glimmer of burnished sacrifice in such friendship. Men have climbed the Golden Stairs for less than that. But temptation! Take Pat away from Marse Henry and the Colonel, and old Beck? What if something happened to her? It was up to me to hesitate, but I lost. The former joys of breaking my own great dogs, gone these several seasons— and now—opportunity to train a grand ten month's beauty for Marse Henry. It was just too good to be true. Two weeks later, traveling like a queen, in state, Pat came to Dixie. Sixty pounds of sleek Chesapeake Bay, and a credit to her blood and raising. A bit timid after the long ride, and naturally homesick for the farm and her folks. But, when she found Miss Irma loved her just as much as she had our own big Pat dog, and that she had the run of the house and could ride alongside her mistress and bark out of the car window as loud as she pleased—why, everything became just right. We took her to our duck club, a comfortable shack alongside a lake full of wildfowl foods and cypress trees. There she came to know Big and Little Jim and Lelia, the folks who mind the place, and Buck and Ball, the coon hounds. What a watch dog she became, and what a pet. On hand for a game of "hide me something" the moment we arrived. Some member's slipper to be hunted down, an orange or apple to be pulled off the tall mantel, or a boisterous romp that completely un-bedded the dormitory.

At first, Pat was a bit boat shy. I have seen other Chesapeake pups the same way. But before long she found out what such affairs were all about, and thereafter promptly and possessively manned the front over-deck. Her first "duck" was an old boxing glove, about the size of a bird, and of a texture to make her tender mouthed. From the boat, I'd toss the glove far into some tall cover, shoot the gun and bid her "bring!" This process was repeated day after day, and then reversed, the glove being thrown from a blind across open water. Later, a mud hen, caught in a muskrat trap and badly hurt, became Pat's first blood and feathers. Through all Pat's primer days the flight was coming down. Overnight our lake was reloaded with mallards, sprigs, teal, widgeon, shovellers and gadwall.

Opening day, at last! I was shooting that morning with my cousin. Pat evinced a lively interest in everything en route to the blind. When great bunches of quacking mallards leaped as our boat rounded some narrow trail, she squirmed and whined. She had ducks in her blood, all right, and knew there was "something shaking." Looking back at me and my gun, she literally licked her chops. There was that noise due, Pat was figuring. While I waded about placing the "blocks," Pat solemnly inspected each one. But when I weighted and tossed out the first live caller, there was a hullaballoo. In two leaps that sent water flying, she was on top of the shrieking mallard. But a new tone in my shout of "Let it alone," stopped her instantly. Looking straight at me, as though thinking it all out for a moment, she released the struggling drake and marched meekly to the boat. Never again did she pay the slightest attention to a live decoy.

By six forty-five, all was ready. Seven o'clock is "union" shooting hour at our duck dub, so a fifteen minute interval of delicious agony had to be endured. Hundreds of ducks, routed from our big pond, returned; the air and water were atwinkle. Pat stationed herself on the boat's prow, just behind the elbow brush. She was strictly at attention. A handsome mallard, our first customer, was just ahead of three more swinging over adjacent timber. We let him glide straight in and alight. The others circled once and dropped in against a faint breeze. These we bagged, and Ev, with his remaining barrel, accounted for the original incomer. At the report of our guns I was conscious of Pat's taking a header off her station and buck-jumping toward a flapping bird. She hesitated at first, just as she had done with the poule d'eau, but after a sniff or two, picked up the victim, and with head and tail erect made a perfect retrieve of her first real mallard. Depositing her pick-up, she licked its bedraggled plumage a bit, shook herself furiously, and then smiled up at me. I tossed an empty shell toward a second victim. Instantly she caught the suggestion and was on her way. The sport from then on was fast and furious. I let Pat do as she pleased, and she was plenty busy. When time was up she had piled the better part of two limits into the boat. She was a "natural." All that fall her water and wildfowl and gun lessons continued. I used her for geese on the sand bars and had her follow me wading through overflowed timber. Pat made few failures at spotting shot-down birds under such acid test. Just before Christmas I shipped her to Marse Henry and wrote him I thought she "had everything" and would retrieve anything that was loose at both ends. In January, with Pat one year old, I returned to the Potomac for some duck shooting with Marse Henry and Doc. He has his own particular hunting system and methods of working out results. And he gets them, too. He had figured it all out, and reset his blind on the tip of a shore point. To its left, the big river "coves," and a right wind swings up-comers in much closer for stooling. Half a mile or so above, the shallow expanse of Broad Creek lets in, a great rafting place for feeders. Behind the blind a belt of heavy woodland thickens down-shore, into a tangle of low shrubs, vines and beach boulders. Off the abrupt bank, a plank walk extends out to the box, perfectly camouflaged, even down around its ankles, with cedar boughs. Four-foot piling allows for tidal variance. Inside are cushioned seats, shell and gun racks, an oil heater for each end, and a heavy tarp cover that can be used as a laprobe to hold in heat during bitter weather. A twelve-inch plank, set at just the right angle, catches the wind and tosses it overhead. "I've found out," said Marse Henry, "that in my own home blind I might just as well be reason-ably comfortable—we have to do all our own chores around here anyhow, and there is plenty of grief outside the box." Marse Henry is right about that. When you hunt with him you do a man's work somehow or other. There's plenty of room for six gunners and all three of those big Chesa-peakes, Fritz, Pat and old Mamma Beck. "Maybe three brown bears is too much of a crowd" continues Marse Henry, "but they're company for me and the Colonel—I like to fool with 'em and watch Beck teach 'em tricks of her trade." Three retrievers in a boat or any other blind than Henry's would be worse than trying to manage four prima donnas in the same opera troupe. But at his place, well, things are just different—even to the actual shooting. Somehow, when the cans rip off from lines winging up-Potomac half a mile out, and make a dart to look you over—you had better make arrangements to do business on a brisk basis. Because, as my old but observing friend, Horace Miller, would comment: "Dem birds acts so brief." From the jump you might just as well begin at a true forty yards and figure outward. I have shot ducks at many a place and under widely varying conditions, but Marse Henry's is where the diplomas are really handed out. Acquire one there, take 'em as they come, and you can slide up to the firing line at any duck-shooting counter in these United

States and "take out a stack," feeling reasonably qualified regardless of what you're up against.

That first day there were five of us in the box—Marse Henry, the Colonel, Ira, Doc and I. The Colonel was merely visiting, and Ira was having his gunning helping Doc with the picture machine. I think Pat knew me. She put her paws on my shoulders, stared me straight in the eyes, and grinned. Then she sniffed my jacket carefully, and ended by trying to push me over backward with face lickings. There was a fine flight, that day. At the crack of our guns, out would bounce all three dogs, with Beck invariably first. Fritz held up his end in good shape, but, to my amazement and chagrin, Pat more or less hung back. With three or four birds down amid wind and wave, three dogs have plenty of work cut out for them. "What's the matter with her?" I asked, when several times she held back, or starting rather grudgingly, turned shoreward. "Why, you'd think she'd never seen a duck, much less retrieved one." Marse Henry's brow wrinkled. "I don't know," he parried—"I think she's all right basically, or that she'll develop—maybe after your way of shooting down there, she hasn't 'savvied' this deep water stuff—maybe she's depending too much on the old bitch."

But I couldn't exactly figure it out that way. Fritz was out on his own, but all Pat would do was run around in circles. It depressed me terribly after what I'd seen the animal accomplish down home. It was in her, right enough. Why, I had pictures of her retrieving, putting ducks into our boat. I could prove it by Harold, or Irma. Harold could tell 'em about that day, for instance, when I banged down a timber scraper that Pat chased clean across the pond and into the big cypress. And on her way back she spotted an overlooked drifter and fetched in a double. And that goose she chased to midriver of the Mississippi and brought in like nobody's business. Something was wrong, somewhere. I grew afraid Marse Henry might think I'd been spoofing him just because Pat was his dog. It wasn't much of a day, on Pat's account. Nor did succeeding shoots prove any more satisfactory. Duck season was running out. I waxed almost morose on the subject of Pat's fall-down. She was alert enough, bat compared to the animal I'd worked down home, she apparently didn't know what it was all about. Was Pat yellow? Impossible! Brainless? Certainty not! Why, she was a sweetheart, and smart as a steel trap. Lazy? Not Pat, of all dogs, with that mother of hers, and the stunts I'd seen her pull off. All I could do was wait, and while nature was taking its course, try to puzzle out the thing.

Last day of the wildfowling calendar! One that shook its fist in our faces and flung a dare to do something about it. Offshore, a quarter mile of milling ice; even the steamer channel was full of heavy floes. Great fields splitting loose from the mouth of Broad Creek and crunching past with a grinding roar that kept us shifting desperately to salvage decoy strings. Inshore the tide-groaning masses piled into towering bergs that fell of their own weight and formed fantastic caves. But our outfit's battle with such elements won and earned its last day's fun. What birds we killed gave Beck a trying time of it. Son Fritz had managed to wire-cut himself and was in the sick bay. Pat was on hand, but of little if any help. She was as affectionate as ever, but somehow palpably shy of it all. Her whole attitude was that of a human being trying, beneath some complex, to grope at the past for spiritual urge.

It was coming good sundown, with first pink and then a darker gloam mantling Virginia's shoreline. Up and down river distant guns were reluctantly booming hunter's fond farewell to governmental regulation. While Marse Henry and Doc loaded a share of the duffle and birds through the woods copse, I set about battening down the blind's tarpaulin. What a gorgeous after-flare from reflecting ice to sky. "Look your last, you gunners," it seemed to say; "today will soon belong to the log-book—say a prayer for the tomorrow that is hope." An edged wind gnawed at my stiffening fingers. My gun leaned against a snag. Suddenly, down river, across the cove, three shadows blotted a fading patch of ocher east and winked silently our way. Crouching, I snatched my weapon. Black duck! A long way out, but by thunder, I'd have a go at that big center fellow if it was the last shot I ever made.

A dog sprang noiselessly down from the overhead bank and hunkered alongside. I was afraid to take my eyes off the approaching birds. Couldn't be Fritz. A quick, closer scrutiny. Not Beck—her nose and eyebrows were graying. Why—a stabbing blade of hope—it—it—was—Pat. I felt her quiver and heard a faint, eager whine that took me back to sand bars and swamps and boat prows and tall timber. I sensed her lemon eyes ashine, and fixed—with intent to kill. Renewed affection surged through me. This was her game and mine again—together—the kind she'd learned. No more confinement in the blind—the gun—the game—everything in sight. The complex went glimmering.

A swinging lead, and heavy tubes spat a gash across the wind-whistle. The big center duck tumbled. Beating the gun, Pat—the real Pat now—lunged—showering me with muddy gravel as she clawed plungingly out onto the ice field. With a fifty-yard start, her crippled quarry was fluttering toward the distant open channel and safety. Realization of danger swept over me. Bad business out there—for boat or man—much less a dog. Out where the jam ended, a treacherous coating of shaved snow—and off it relentless floes that would drill a yawl. "Come back, Pat," I yelled, rushing after her until I broke through the crust and into boot-deep eddy. "Pat—Pat—here—here—come back." Far out on the ice a racing dot grew smaller and smaller—lost to sight against distant hills. Then I knew. Seeing me crouched there, it had all swept back to her—images from a dream time. In that brief moment, memory flashed of old Beck's bearing Pat's unborn spirit through icy travail. Men are said to "find themselves." Why not a dog?

And then, as night flung suddenly down, out there among waves and the creaking smash of sullen turmoil, Pat disappeared. Marse Henry was alongside by now, listening to the story and calling, with me, out across the gloom. Fifteen, twenty minutes passed. Our voices hoarsened against the tumult, with something dreadfully pathetic tugging at our hearts. A shred of moonlight tipped the crest of Maryland and swathed the river's shroud with pallid paths. And into its widening beneficence, from behind an ice barrier far to our left, crept an almost ghostly, slow-walking Pat. Pat grizzly with frozen spray, but head and tail erect, with a live, unrumpled black duck between her jaws. Marse Henry's eyes and my own met in unutterable relief—and something much, much more. Into our hearts had surged not alone gratitude for Pat's restoration, or a mere coming into her own. Just the choky tribute of silence, a palm from two hard-bitten duck shooters to a dog's flaming courage and unspeakable devotion.

## CHAPTER 7

# A Drink for the Dog

By Tom Hennessey

*WE INTRODUCED TOM IN AN EARLIER CHAPTER, "HOMEBODIES." IN THIS PIECE, also excerpted from his book* Feathers 'n Fins *(1989), we're going duck hunting with Tom and his chocolate Lab, Coke, on the rugged Maine coast. Always dangerous, the hunting there can quickly turn into a life-threatening experience.*

It was a little past 9 A.M. when I turned off the Gouldsboro Point Road and pulled into Galen's yard. Leaning forward, I opened the door of the pickup and Coke, my chocolate Lab retriever, bounded out of the cab. When Galen came out the back door of his house, Gib, his young black Lab retriever, charged ahead of him and immediately the dogs began romping about the premises.

After we had loaded a skiff into the back of my truck and piled our duck hunting gear into it, Galen and I went into the house to wait for Mike, Kenny, Lewis and Gary to show up. We had a little time to kill. The tides had worked around to where high water would occur about 1 P.M. It would be half tide—around 10 o'clock—before we could rig our decoys off the point where we planned to shoot.

While we sipped steaming cups of coffee, Coke and Gib raced past the windows, tumbling and snarling in mock anger. By the time the others arrived, both dogs were puffing and panting in good shape. I should have had the presence of mind to give Coke a drink of water right then. But in our anxiety to get to the gunning grounds we piled into two trucks and rumbled out of the yard. Because Galen's Gib was, at the time, plagued with a leg-muscle problem that cold water would aggravate, he was left home. The retrieving chores would be handled by Coke and Lewis's Bear, a black Lab pup that was showing a lot of promise.

For late-season duck shooting, the day was made to order. Shafts of sunlight sliced through layers of leaden clouds, and the breeze brisking up with the tide bobbed the decoys at the ends of their anchor lines. It was one of those once-in-a-while times when you could feel it in your bones that everything was just right.

We split into two groups. Galen, Gary, Coke, and I in a blind on one side of the point. Mike, Kenny, Lewis, and Bear on the other side. Hardly had we loaded our shotguns when Galen warned, "Watch it—buffleheads!" In diving-duck fashion—low and fast—they wheeled in and buzzed the formally dressed black and white decoys. When Galen and I hauled down, three ducks folded and spanked the surface. Gary was biding his time for black ducks. After fetching the buffleheads, Coke, to my shock and surprise, went to the water's edge and began drinking.

"No!" I yelled. He stopped, but then and there the damage was done. Shortly after, as he retrieved a drake whistler, I could hear Coke gulping salt water as he swam. With salt in his system his thirst became insatiable. When he came ashore his belly was bulging and I knew it would be only a matter of minutes before he'd be sick. The big retriever vomited violently. Water came out of him as though a fire hydrant had been uncapped. To my surprise, as soon as Coke had rid himself of the briny bellywash he seemed to be in good spirits. Wagging his tail, he bounded over to me and took my wrist in his mouth—his usual greeting and signal that all is well. It wasn't. As many times as we had hunted the coastal marshes, Coke had never attempted to drink salt water. I realized that the roughhouse romping with Galen's pup had overheated him, and I cursed myself for not having taken the time to give him a drink before we left.

The rush of primary feathers ripping air announced the arrival of a pair of black ducks. On set wings they scaled toward the dozen black duck decoys that we had set off separately to our right. A charge of No. 4 shot from Gary's long-barreled 12-gauge hauled feathers from the duck nearest us and it planed away in a long slanting dive. A white plume leaped from the surface as the wounded black struck far out in the bay. It would be a long, tiring retrieve, and as Coke churned after the diving, sculling duck I again heard him drinking.

Damn! How could I have been so negligent?

Swimming ashore slowly, the dog dropped the duck when he waded onto the gravelly point. Again the water gushed out of him. This time, however, he didn't run to me with assurances that he felt fine. This time he did what I had never seen him do in four years of hunting. He lay down.

There was no need to tell Galen and the others that I was done hunting. Quickly we took up the decoys. Quickly we gathered our gear, and quickly we lit out of there. At Galen's house Coke drank a bowl of water dry and then curled up on the truck seat as we headed for Hampden. About the time we were driving through Holden, the dog began to get uneasy. Sitting up, he tilted his nose upward and breathed heavily. At home I immediately called the Penobscot Veterinary Hospital. "Bring him out," said Dr. Meiczinger after I had explained the situation.

"Will he be okay?" I asked as the vet poked two large pink pills down Coke's throat. "He'll be okay," was the welcome reply. "All that salt water was a shock to his system," Dr. Meiczinger continued, "that plus vomiting dehydrated him, took all the starch out of him. I'll give him a couple of shots that will help stabilize his system, then I'll need some X-rays to make sure there isn't any water in his abdomen." I noticed that Coke was breathing easier. The pills, the vet explained, had soothed the dog's intestinal tract which was raw and inflamed from the salt water. That was why Coke had tilted his nose upward. In that position the tract straightened and he could swallow air easier in an attempt to put out the fire.

No water showed in the X-rays. Dr. Meiczinger then informed me that he was going to start Coke on intravenous feeding and keep him overnight. "This guy needs some nutrition," he said. "Call me about nine in the morning and we'll see how things are shaping up." With that thought-provoking hook-up of bottle, tube and needle attached to his right foreleg I left Coke in a kennel and went out into the dark.

Driving home, the thought drummed in my mind: all this for lack of a drink of water.

I wasn't popular at home. It wasn't bad enough that I felt as if I had betrayed my best friend; now my wife and kids were looking at me as if I'd spent the Christmas Club money on a new outboard motor. All that night I lay awake wondering how the best gun dog I've ever owned was getting along. He seemed so weak and lifeless when I left him. Would he really be all right? What if, somehow, the intravenous tube and needle became separated with the needle remaining in the dog's vein? Would he lose blood, or, worse, bleed to death? It was a long night.

Next morning, however, my worries were put to rest. Although still weak and wrung out, Coke was well enough to go home. For two days he ate and drank very little. When I spoke to him he would manage only one or two thumps of his tail. Seeing that big, burly dog in that condition depressed me and the thought plagued me—if I'd had water with me that never would have happened.

It upset and worried me that Coke wouldn't eat. No matter what I put in front of him, he refused it. Now it just so happened that my wife had roasted a turkey, and I remembered Coke actually drooling whenever a roast turkey appeared on the kitchen countertop. I went to the refrigerator and sliced off a slab of white meat. Coke ate it. In the next day or so, in fact, he ate that whole turkey, down to the last scrap of golden-brown skin. That seemed to be the turning point. The dog began eating regularly and in a week's time had bounced back to almost 100 percent.

After that unpleasant experience I vowed I would never again gun the coastal marshes without bringing along a drink for the dog. A retriever is sure to swallow some water while fetching ducks and you're well aware of the thirst that just a small piece of salty ham or corned beef can create. A quart plastic jug full of water and a small plastic bowl aren't much to lug in a pack basket, and you can bet your retriever will be mighty glad you brought it along if he or she develops a powerful thirst. Look at it this way: it might keep you from losing a night's sleep and a roast turkey dinner.

## CHAPTER 8

# My Most Memorable Dog

### By Archibald Rutledge

*THIS EDITOR HAS ALWAYS LOOKED UPON THE WORKS OF ARCHIBALD RUTLEDGE (1883–1973) with great awe. His prose and poetry set in the South Carolina Lowcountry call out the life I spent as a youth in southeast Georgia. My days afield could not match the great Archibald Rutledge adventures from Hampton and the Santee River area, but I found much reading that bonded me with Mr. Rutledge. Poet laureate of South Carolina and author of so many stories and books too lengthy to mention in the limited space here, Rutledge was a man who led two lives. In one life he grew up on Hampton Plantation and returned there for lengthy Christmas vacations every year. His other life was as an English professor at Mercersburg Academy in Pennsylvania. His years of hunting experience were as diverse as bobwhite quail and ruffed grouse. This Rutledge classic was presented in my friend Jim Casada's book* Bird Dog Days, Wingshooting Ways *(2016), a bountiful collection of Rutledge upland hunting stories. It includes the best short biography of Archibald Rutledge I've ever seen.*

During the years of my young manhood, when I was a teacher in the beautiful Cumberland Valley of Pennsylvania, I hunted quail and grouse a great deal, and I raised and trained a good many bird dogs.

Animals can occasionally be as memorable as human beings; among dogs I give the first place to Mike. Although he was no beauty, he was a joy forever. There was a pathos about him as if he were aware of his unpromising looks.

In those early years I inevitably hunted quail but finally gave it up, for I love the birds too much. One year I went quite overboard in buying a registered pointer with the proud name of Savannah Count. He arrived in a crate that looked like a palace. He was huge, handsome, and supercilious. For some reason, he seemed especially oblivious to me.

On the first day of the season I took His Majesty into the fields. At the first shot he vanished over the rolling countryside. The lordly Count was gun-shy. I did not retrieve him for days.

I was reminded of a dog I took to old Galboa to correct the same fault. Galboa was a native African who had a way with animals. Telling the old man my troubles, I left the dog with him for two weeks. When I returned, he gestured with contempt toward the dog lying in the grass. "You must learn," he said, "that nothing can be done about a fool."

There are few plights worse for a quail hunter than to have no bird dog when the season opens. When Count defected, I at once called up a Pennsylvania Game protector, a good friend of mine, to ask him if he could relieve my emergency. He raised bird dogs "on the side," and I had bought several good ones from him. But his report was disappointing. "I did have two dandies," he said, "but I sold both last week. I haven't got a thing now but Mike, and I don't like to sell him to you. You and I have been good friends."

Although this seemed like a sinister introduction, I said, "Ship him to me." As if to sink Mike even lower in my estimation, my friend said, "I could not charge you more than $15.00 for this mutt." (I had paid $100.00 for my airborne Savannah Count.)

When Mike arrived, I found him, in appearance, no "hound of heaven." Undersized, angular, with bristly red and yellow hair, for a bird dog he appeared to be put together wrong. His ears were small and peaked; someone had cut off more than half his tail. No one had lately taken him to a beauty parlor. But, as a judge once said to me, about the possible verdict of a jury, "Brother, you never know."

As if he had everything else against him, Mike's feet were too large, so that he walked as if he had snowshoes on. Despite all these adverse factors, Mike had qualities to admire, and, for me, a human and lovable nature. He had a good head, which should presage wisdom and a keen nose. Mike had, too, like some people, a certain air about him; an ugly air, but unique and unforgettable.

Of course, Mike had not any social background. To gracious living, he was alien. Yet already I could feel his loyalty to me. He was also courageous. As I led him up to my home, which was near the express office, we met a big dog that I knew to be a mean one. The big dog, bristling, made some invidious remarks about Mike's mother. Mike bristled also, took a step forward, growling. He was ready for a fight.

I never learned anything of Mike's ancestry; but somewhere in it a blooded pointer probably could be found. He looked to be all cur; but there was something about him that made me know that he wasn't. He had ways and wiles about him.

I have owned many good dogs, but Mike was a character. He was always surprising me with the things he did, which he had thought out all by himself, things that endeared him to me. For example, one afternoon we were crossing a field when we came to a rather cold dark stream with steep banks. Mike did not like the looks of it; but his heart must have kept saying, "Whither thou goest, I will go." I managed to slip down the bank, cross the water with the aid of some limbs, and literally crawled up the farther bank. I then looked for Mike and called him.

Having estimated the problem, and disliking cold water, he had calmly walked away from the creek in a straight line, just as a high jumper or a pole vaulter would, in order to afford himself a speedy run for his takeoff. He went about thirty yards, turned, and came running full speed for the creek. There was a break in the trees so that I could watch him land safely. I was surprised how high he went.

A wild white-tailed deer has been known to jump forty-two feet; a horse, thirty-six feet; a man, twenty-eight feet. I am sure that Mike jumped between twenty and twenty-five feet, and he did so with certainty and grace.

The same week I took a friend hunting quail. Every time he shot, he missed. Meanwhile Mike disappeared. I was not surprised, as his russet coloring blended perfectly with those of the autumn. When I found him he was lying flat in a ditch, his head on his outstretched paws. He looked at me with eyes that seemed to express disappointment, chagrin, and even disgust. He was not able to take any more strong doses of missing! It made him sick; besides, all his work was going for nothing. Of course, I may have misinterpreted his expression; but it looked like humiliating regret to me. Indeed, Mike's expression was so forlorn it would not have surprised me if big dash tears had rolled down his cheeks.

As we approached an old rail fence one day, Mike sprang up to the top rail. It must have been at that moment that one of the top rails began to swing at right angles to the line of the fence. Just at that moment the hot and heavy scent of a covey of quail, almost beneath him, assailed Mike's nostrils. He crept forward a step to make certain, and found himself with all four feet on the swaying fence rail. Mike's game was to keep his balance and also not to frighten the covey. I can still see him, the picture of shrewd loyalty and devotion, holding his balance until I could come up. He was rocking perfectly.

On another occasion I missed him. After a few minutes he came creeping and crawling back to me. On reaching me, he whined, turned around and started back the way he had come. He paused, looking back to make sure I understood his message and was following. His gait was very peculiar. He was walking as if he were stepping on eggs. He led me to a big covey of quail. He must have known that I could not see him; so he came and got me!

One day Mike and I were out on a sandy road when a big crowd of frolicking young people came by. Purely in jest, one of them threw a pine cone at Mike. It did not hit him; but even if it had, it could not have hurt him. But it wounded his dignity; and he never forgot it.

Except for the one who threw the cone, all the others could enter my yard in perfect safety. But the one who threw the cone would stop outside the gate and call for someone please to "tie Mike up." Really gentle by disposition, Mike would not let anyone take liberties with him.

When I hunted in Pennsylvania, there were some ringneck pheasants there. We were allowed to kill only the cock birds, which are easily distinguished by their gaudy colors and their long tails. It is characteristic of these birds that they will often run long distances on the ground before taking flight. One afternoon, in a wild valley, Mike struck a trail. I knew at once it must be a pheasant because of the distance he was going. At last he came to a stand. I walked carefully to flush the bid. After all our long walk, it was a hen! Of course, I did not shoot. As I stood idly there, Mike, apparently in anger, whirled on me and barked in the most disgusted fashion! There was no mistaking what he meant: "After all my careful work, what in the world is the matter with you?" Some dogs are certainly capable of rebuking their masters—if the provocation is great.

Once when Mike and I were hunting in a field of wheat stubble near a thicket of blackberry canes, he came back to me whining, and he seemed to be cringing. Something had scared him, and he was not a dog easily scared. I was wearing my corduroy trousers; and he took hold of the cuff of one leg, to pull me back, or at least to delay me. But feeling I should investigate, I literally dragged Mike through the stubble. As we drew near the briar patch, I heard what had frightened Mike; then I saw the snake, that ashen heap of death. I have lost dogs that have been struck by rattlers, and have located these lethal serpents by dogs which barked at them—being wary enough to keep their distance. I looked at Mike. In his eyes was a distinct warning. I had dealt with dogs all my life, but what kind of a dog was this? I have had a good dog "take on" a wild boar that had personal designs on me. Yet I doubt if that brave dog was really defending me. With Mike it was different. He cautiously warned me against what he knew was deadly danger. Is it any wonder that I love and honor his memory?

Early in our acquaintance he gave me a good idea of his unusualness. Early one damp morning, I drove out in a buggy (I had no car) to hunt quail. Mike lay in the bottom of the buggy and a robe covered him and my knees. About a mile from town a heavy Osage orange hedge stood on the left of the road. As we were passing this, something happened—something for which I could not at first account. The robe had risen off my knees. Mike was standing up. As soon as I saw the trance-like look in his eyes, I knew that he had winded quail, and had pointed them from the buggy! For precaution's sake, I drove forward a few paces, where I got out of the buggy. But as he was still pointing, I had to lift him down to the roadway. He was still pointing, and as stiff as a board.

When his feet touched the ground he began a curious stiff-legged walk back down the road. Then he came to a perfect point. As the grass was rather thin, I saw the quail on the ground, a beautiful covey of about sixteen birds. When they rose and whirled over the hedge, I did not shoot—partly, I think, because of the strange magic of Mike's behavior.

On another occasion I took a friend duck hunting. Flight shooting was then permitted after sundown. I put my friend on a good stand and he blazed away for an hour. I shot only twice. But when dark came, and I started down the old bank on which we had been standing, I almost fell over a big pile of wild ducks. That was Mike's work. He had brought all my friend's ducks to me! He had original ideas about loyalty.

When the Great Depression came, I had three sons in college. I had already sold some heirloom furniture. Was there anything else that might bring in some money? There was Mike. Unfortunately a man of means had seen him work. He had several times approached me to buy him. Meanwhile the university treasurer kept bearing down on me. On a disastrous day I decided to let my dear Mike go. I felt worse than a sinner. While I was making the crate, Mike watched me curiously. When I put him in and nailed it shut, he must have had an inkling of what was coming. He lay flat on the bottom of the box, and looked at me with big misty eyes. I set the crate in the wheelbarrow, and rolled it down to the express office. I heard some subdued whimpering, but I really believe that Mike was weeping. Nor was he the only one. I left him at the office to be shipped out.

But I had hardly reached home when the enormity of my crime overcame me. I rushed back to the express office (although no train was due for several hours). "It's a mistake!" I exclaimed to the express agent. "I'm not going to sell him."

Not long after that I decided to stop quail shooting. By then Mike was getting old. The aspect of the approach of age is always sad with a dog as active and intelligent as Mike. While he was still strong, I could expect him always to meet me halfway down the avenue that led to my home. He apparently timed my arrival; but was usually an hour or so early, just lying there waiting. At other times, he would pull at my corduroy trousers, trying to get me started on a hunt, or would run down the avenue, barking, and looking expectantly toward the house for me to join him. But then came days when he did not meet me. And sometimes when I would seem to be getting ready to go for a hunt, he would lie in the sun by the steps, thump the ground with his tail, and look at me with a nameless wistfulness. He seemed to be acknowledging his own weakness, and doing so with tragic regret. His eyes spoke for him. Like King Lear, he was saying, "I am old now."

Then, too, Mike began to make mistakes in the field. One day he was holding a point on the briared bank of a ditch. I was sure he had a quail or a pheasant. But as I got near him he gave up the point, and turned back to me, his expression registering shame and apology. He crawled up to me whining, and rubbed against my boots, as if imploring forgiveness. He was abashed that he had been pointing an old land turtle! Yet the finest part of his life was yet to come. He had always loved children, and had been a great favorite with them. One of my grandsons was crazy about Mike; when, therefore, the boy's mother told me that another child was expected, I let them take him. "He might make a nurse for the baby." I said, never dreaming of the real import of my words.

In a pretty room on the second floor of my son's house all was made ready for the new baby. In the center of the room was the immaculate crib, all lacy and frilly. There was a mahogany footboard around the base. One day when the mother came into the room she was greeted by a low growl. Mike had taken possession of the little square box beneath the bassinet. Please don't ask me how he knew a baby was coming there. Perhaps he had dealt with a baby before, in another family. True, there was an unwonted air of suppressed excitement and expectancy, and he may have interpreted these. Do some animals, at certain times, have the eerie clairvoyance of premonition? At any rate, Mike planted himself under the bassinet, and would not leave. He had to be fed and watered there.

The mother was at the hospital two weeks. When she brought the tiny daughter home, Mike barked delightedly. And he took charge. Except for the mother, he would let no one else enter the room. When the baby cried, or even fretted, Mike barked. After some months had passed, and the baby began to crawl about the room, Mike would come close and lie down so that tiny Bonnie could sleep with him for a pillow. My daughter-in-law said, "I feel much safer with Mike than with a nurse."

When Bonnie was a year and a half old, she was allowed to run up and down the pavement in front of her house—but only if Mike went with her. He was not by then keeping up with the baby very well. He always stayed between her and the street. One day she threw a little rubber ball out into the road, and at once, like a fairy, ran after it. Mike was old then and not nearly so fast as he had once been. Two cars were coming from opposite directions, Mike, making the effort of his life, dashed between Bonnie and one car. She was saved, but he was struck and killed.

Mike was a dog that looked all wrong, but was all right. Ugly, he was loyal and smart. Many redeeming faults were his—those same human qualities that make people lovable. It is not hard for me to forget Savannah Count; but I shall always remember Mike.

## Chapter 9

# The Tail-Ender

By Henry P. Davis

*GOOD FOX-HUNTING STORIES HAVE BECOME ABOUT AS RARE AS GOOD FOX-hounds in this modern age, but they are still treasured in much of the hunting community. This story by Henry P. Davis (1894–1970) appeared in the now-defunct* Outdoorsman *magazine and was collected in the anthology* Outdoors Unlimited *(1947), edited by J. Hammond Brown.*

There are two kinds of people in my home town: those who fox-hunt—and those who don't. The latter class is not very popular. New-comers receive a cordial welcome, for we are hospitable folks. But the news that they have moved into a foxhunting community is imparted in a polite, roundabout, but quite definite way.

Cap'n Jeff, the official greeter, will say, "We're glad to have you folks among us. We'll try to make you feel at home and we hope you'll be happy here. If you happen to hear, and I reckon you will, a pack of hounds running sometimes late at night, don't let it bother you. It's just us fox-hunters having some fun. And we'd be mighty glad to have you join us." That's the official invitation—and the only one ever extended.

Take it or leave it. If the invitation is accepted, all well and good. All courtesies possible are extended. If no interest is shown or weak excuses made, there is no lessening of hospitality, but the head of the house finds himself outside the "inner circle" until, as many do, he "tries out" foxhunting. Once inoculated, he generally becomes one of the regulars.

There are three kinds of foxhunters in my home town: foxhunters who are everything the name implies, owning their own hounds and hunting them; foxhunters who sit on their front porches and listen to the hound chorus as it ebbs and flows across the countryside—and "joiners."

Which brings us around to Tal Murray. Old Tal Murray, a self-effacing landmark in our community, who did much for many without thought of credit to himself. No one knows how much. Nobody even gives it a thought. But just bring up his name in the nightly drugstore conversation and there comes to every old-timer present a smile, a skipped heartbeat, the memory of "Tail-ender." For Tal Murray owned Tail-ender, a hound well remembered in our community. Some called him great. Well remembered in our community means the same thing.

Tal and Tail-ender embodied the spirit of the chase—and a man's love for, and pride in, his dog. For a good many reasons, Tal had been a "joiner." He had no hounds of his own, but no matter in what section we hunted he would generally turn up. We got so we sort of listened for the "clopaclopclop" of the little bay mare he called his "noddin' hoss" when the hunt was up and the going good. He always timed his arrival properly. When the race was on and everyone was in high fettle and "joiners" were welcome, someone would say, "Well, I reckon old Tal'll be along d'rectly." Sure enough, presently around the bend would come the nodding head of bay Ella, with Tal sitting straight as an Indian in the saddle. As he eased alongside he'd invariably say, "Jumped him, ain't yuh?"

Yes, Tal was always welcome. Quiet, unobtrusive and understanding, he said little and what he did say was kindly, considerate and encouraging. No matter whose dog was leading, to Tal the pack was always "right." No man loved foxhunting more and he knew every foot of the country for miles around. So we often wondered why he didn't a have hound or two of his own. Why his abundant praise was lavished on our hounds instead of some who ate his own pot-licker. No one chided him about it, for, as I say, Tal was always welcome.

One night Tal was late. Old Red had been giving our hounds merry hell, and vice versa, for more than an hour when we came upon him. As we topped the highest point on Devil's Backbone, Tal was standing by a rock in the moonlight, Ella tethered placidly, but attentively, nearby.

Sharply silhouetted against a background of moonlight, Tal was listening to mellow music made by the four-footed chorus which swung up and over and through the rough country below. Mumbling to himself, we thought. Then we saw that at his side crouched a dog, eager of ears and tail a-wag.

"By Joe," said one. "Old Tal's got hisse'f a houn'."

And sure enough he had. Tal was immediately overwhelmed with banter of one sort or another—congratulatory and otherwise. But with all our rough talk we were genuinely interested, and he knew it. So he let us have our fling. And what a fling we had! No one listened to the race that was going on, hammer and tongs, in the valley below us. Forgotten was the argument about whether Jimminy Cricket or Martha was leading the pack. Forgotten was everything except Old Tal has a hound!

The Colonel took no part in our chatter. Just sat on his horse and looked at Tal's hound. For, time after time, he had offered old Tal his pick of a litter and I guess he was just about as curious as we were.

With nod of his head he called me to him and whispered, "Kick up a fire and we'll look at Mr. Murray's hound. I think he'd like to tell us about him."

We didn't need a fire for warmth, although the night was cool. But there is something about a fire in the open, daytime or night, that draws folks, makes them sort of thaw out, physically, mentally and conversationally.

As the flickering flame mingled with moonbeams melting through the scrub oak everybody, including Tal, gathered 'round.

He came in and stood—with a raw-boned young hound at his side. I won't forget the sight, for moonlight threw the shadows of both across us all. Even across my puny little fire, Tal had the spotlight tonight. The dog seemed to sense, too, that he was the focus point of all eyes. He shrank against Tal's booted leg and stood with lowered flag and quivering muscles.

There was both apology and pride in Tal's voice as he spoke his piece. "Wal, y'all seem to wonder 'bout this here pup," he said, "so reck'n I'd better tell you 'bout him. I've wanted a real fox dog fur a long time so I could reely feel like I was one of you fellers when I joined up with you these nights. Wanted to git my dog in my own way. Never seemed to find one to suit. Till t'other day that hoss trader feller, that comes through here twice a year and camps in pasture, turned into my road lookin' like a cucus peerade. Had a span of spangled calicos pullin' his waggin and strung out behind it was fo'teen head of the dangest lookin' hoss-flesh y'ever seen. All but two or three were jus' plain snides.

"At the tail end of the procession, this here young houn' come a-trottin' along, proud and purty as a prize punkin. An' I said right there 'That's the houn' I'm a-lookin' fur.'

"So the fust thing I know that hoss trader feller had that old heavey mare of mine—an' had fo' dollars an' this here houn'. Got papers on him, too, long as a black snake. He come from down in Jefferson county and I figured he'd fit in right well with y'all's pack."

Tal leaned down and stroked the velvet ear of his new possession and waited for our approval—which he promptly got. Our enthusiasm pleased the old fellow mightily and he led his dog out for closer inspection. He was a good looking black and tan, with white points and a white shirt front.

"Tried him out yet?" asked someone.

"Nope," answered Tal. "Thought I'd wait and see how you fellers cottoned to him. Thought mebbe y'all might not like my havin' a houn' that come from aways off."

He was reassured on that point and we were all for putting him in the race that night but Tal begged off. "Ef y'all don't mind," he said, "I'd like to let him just go 'long an' lissen. Sorter git the lay of things, and used to us. That hoss trader feller g'arnteed him as a real fox dog and I shore hope he is. . . . Anyhow, that old heavey wa'nt wuth much more'n fo' dollars."

Business called me away for a while and when I returned the season was on the wane. My first question to the Colonel was, "How's Tal's hound?"

"He'll run, but he won't pack," he said. "Good mouth—and stays. But always behind. As if he is a little bit afraid to fight for the lead. Grand nose. Runs like a streak by himself. Can unravel any check. But he must have been mauled, for he's pack-shy. Always behind—but not far. Remember the night we came across the two of 'em? And Tal said he first saw the dog at the tail-end of the horse trader's troop? Well, he's still in that position in our pack. And the boys have named him—Tail-ender!"

"How does Tal take that?" I asked.

"Oh, you know Tal. He doesn't seem to mind. Thinks that hound is the greatest dog that ever happened. Says he'll show us all some day. And wouldn't be surprised if he does. Hope so, anyway."

The Colonel was very fond of old Tal Murray. Liked his hound, too. He never engaged in the raillery which always followed Tail-ender as he swung by some hundred yards in the rear of the pack. Along toward the end of the season, and even after, for that matter, we all noticed that several times a week he'd saddle Fairy in mid-afternoon and jog away, with one or two couples of old and pensioned hounds at heel. "Just going to give the 'old folks' a little exercise," he'd tell Mother. "But don't wait supper on me." And he always took the lower road which led to Tal Murray's.

I suspected that he and Tal had something on the fire and ventured so far one day as to ask him, "How's Tail-ender coming along? You and Tal must . . ."

He silenced me with a look and said, "Tal may have a surprise for the boys next season."

Four of our bitches spent that summer out at Tal's.

"Thought they might like a change of scenery," the Colonel said by way of explanation. A harem for Tail-ender, I thought. But not out loud.

We gathered in the Sundown Hills for the first meet of the season. Always a gala occasion, the Hell-or-High-Water foxhunting clan really turned out this time. Horseback, muleback, in buggies and afoot, the countryside congregated to partake of the bounty provided by the Colonel and Cap'n Zack and listen to music mankind cannot make.

Black Newby and his helpers, Tobe and Kip, were busy at the barbecue pit, "mopping" the meat of a good sized yearling bull, two goats and a pair of sheep, with juice from the sauce pail, when the Colonel and Cap'n Zack rode up in late afternoon. Esau, the "hound boy," staked his charges out under the hill, away from cantankerous horses and curious kids. The barrel of persimmon beer was tapped and tasted, saddle cinches loosened and all was ready for the frolic. And, in less time than it takes to tell, it began. There was the usual round of greetings as each "joiner" arrived but soon there a was a general settling down to plain and fancy eating of the barbecue and trimmin's.

All the regulars were there—all but Tal. I wondered about that. But soon the moon peeped up over the ridge and gave us a knowing nod, and here came Tal. Astride Ella as usual, with Tail-ender proudly trotting along close by. And at his side was our old limping Fly, who had run the pads off her left hind years ago and about whom I'd almost forgotten. The Colonel had given her to Tal one day saying, "She'll be company for Tail-ender, your dog."

When Tal rode into the grove someone chuckled and said, "Just look at that combination! Old Tal, stumblin' mare, a crippled bitch and a shy dog. Ain't we got fun!" The Colonel smiled, but said nothing.

As Tal dismounted, old Fly caught a glimpse of the picket line below and hobbled down the hill to renew acquaintance with her former kennel mates. Tail-ender trotted along, too. Presently a yell from Esau and a roar from a score or more hounds' throats brought us all to our feet and up running. Tail-ender had our Tattler down. And was giving him— the big boisterous, blustering bully of the pack—the licking of his life! Tail-ender, the shy, was a ball of fire and fury and it took the combined efforts of Esau and Tal to pull him off the chastised Tattler.

"Well, can you beat that?" one said. "The worm has turned! Whatch' been feedin' him, Tal? Gunpowder?" Tal merely smiled.

"Seem lak he makin' up fuh los' time," chuckled Esau. "At Tattluh dawg needed jes' whut he got."

We lingered over the board as the moon came up. Tal and the Colonel were talking together as Tal nibbled on a meaty rib. I eased over and heard the Colonel say in low tones, "We could cast him away first, let him strike and then put the pack in if you'd like, Tal."

The old man smiled and replied, "Thanky, Colonel. But I'd ruther he took his chances with t'others. From the way he jumped Tattler hit looks like our experiment is gonna work."

The Colonel rose. "Let's mount, gentlemen, and see what the night will offer." A short blast on the horn and the pack was straining at the picket line, flags up, eyes eager and mouths a-whine.

They were cast in the valley below us and faded away like silent skirmishers. None was left except old Fly who plodded along by Tal. Presently a roll of music rang from the ridge on the far side of the valley, rippling its liquid note over the open spaces and into the scrub oak hills. "What hound?" asked one. And ten voices cried, "Tail-ender, by gad!"

Tal looked at the Colonel and fairly beamed. "Now we'll see," he said as the pack harked in.

It is only natural for a pack-mauled hound, or one otherwise made shy, to relinquish the lead quickly and willingly, drop back to the rear or even quit entirely when the pack harks in to his strike. We all knew that Tail-ender could run like a tornado when he wanted to. And we all knew that he was, or had been, pack-shy. So we held our breaths as we rode to the crossing and waited for the rolling cascade of music to come back over the hills. We loved and respected old Tal more than he knew and we, to a man, wanted this drama to end happily. Our worries were wasted.

For true to his usual custom, Master Greycoat looped and came straight through "carryin' the mail." Behind him, head up and tail high, reached Tail-ender, in that swinging frictionless gallop which does not recognize fatigue. And behind Tail-ender—behind him, mind you—came the pack, its mixed chorus playing the accompaniment for Tail-ender's solo! Behind him then and behind him all race—for Tail-ender, the shy, had come into his own.

And why not, please? Hadn't he been the boss of his own kennel all summer? Hadn't he licked the bully of the pack? Hadn't he struck and jumped that fox? Wasn't he good as any hound in that pack—or any other pack? You bet—and now he was out to show 'em? And show 'em he did! No dog had his nose in front of Tail-ender that night.

He holed the first fox in an hour and a half. Then jumped another and repeated the performance. In working out checks, in just plain slam-bang-slashing driving there was only one dog in those races that night. Tail-ender. We whopped and yelled and pounded old Tal on the back until he was black and blue. He'd only grin, look at the Colonel and say, "Sorter come inter his own, ain't he?"

It was a grand opening of a grand season, staged and timed perfectly. And it developed that the Colonel was the director of the play.

Wise in the ways of men and animals, he knew that the shyness of Tail-ender and his master, too, was born of a complex termed inferiority. So he set about to correct it, knowing the hidden worth of both. He'd slip over to Tal's with one or two couples of our oldest hounds and run them with the young dog, first allowing Tail-ender to get a fox up and going before he uncoupled the oldsters. Thus the shy one began to gain confidence in his own ability. The trump card in the Colonel's strategy, however, was played when he boarded some of our bitches out at Tal's that summer. This gave Tail-ender a court, made him the cock-of-the-walk and he reacted to this new feeling of importance just as the Colonel expected.

The metamorphosis of Tail-ender became a legend in our country. And brought laurels to Tal the like of which he had never dreamed. He was elected, without opposition, Justice of the Peace in his township and for years meted out justice with Solomon-like wisdom. And Tail-ender was always in the front rank of our pack until old age retired him.

"Jedge" Tailbott Hemingway Murray and his dog, Tail-ender, are gone now, long ago. But their story lives and serves to illustrate the kindly feeling all foxhunters bear for each other. Love of the chase, of fair play, respect and affection for hounds and hills and woods and swamps make kin folks of the foxhunting clan the world over.

## CHAPTER 10

# Old Tantrybogus

By Ben Ames Williams

*THE ROCK-RIBBED MOUNTAINS, HILLS AND VALLEYS OF NEW ENGLAND ARE alive with outdoor adventures throughout the changing seasons. My personal favorites of the tales from that region have always been when bird dogs and their owners were afield in the leaf-changing splendors with ruffed grouse and woodcock on their minds. Ben Ames Williams (1889–1953) could have written about training and handling dogs all his life if he had chosen that path. Instead, he liked stories with drama and action, and he poured all his talents into producing them. This one appeared in his book* Thrifty Stock *(1923), and reading it we are once again afield in the crisp autumn air, watching our dogs work, hoping we can utter or hear that magic word, "Point!"*

# I

To this day, when Chet McAusland tells the tale his voice becomes husky and his eyes are likely to fill—and, "It was murder," he will say when he is done. "I felt like a murderer and that's what I was. But it was too late then." Sometimes his listeners are silent, appearing to agree with him. More often, those to whom he speaks seek to reassure him, for it is plain to any man that there is no murder in Chet, nor any malice nor anything but a very human large-heartedness toward every man and beast.

In Tantry's time Chet was a bachelor living alone at his farm above Fraternity, cooking and caring for himself, managing well enough. He had been a granite cutter, a fisherman upon the Banks, a keeper of bees. Now he farmed his rocky hillside farm. He was a man of middle age—a small man with a firm jaw and a pair of bushy eyebrows and deep-set piercing eyes. When he laughed he had a way of setting his head firmly back upon his neck, his chin pressed down, and his laughter was robust and free and fine. I have spoken of his occupations; he had also avocations. All his life he had fished, had hunted, had traversed the forests far and wide. A man who loved the open, loved the woods, loved the very imprint of a deer's hoof in the mud along the river. A good companion, open-hearted, with never an evil word for any man.

He was, as has been said, a bachelor; but this was not of Chet's own choosing, as at least one person in Fraternity well knew. Old Tantrybogus knew also—knew even in the days when he was called young Job. He knew his mistress as well as he knew his master; knew her as truly as though she dwelt already at the farm upon the hill. Between her and Chet was his allegiance divided. None other shared it ever, even to the end.

Chet as a bachelor kept open house at his farm upon the hill and this was especially true when there was fishing or gunning to be had. A Rockland man came one October for the woodcock shooting. He and Chet found sport together and found—each in the other—a friend. The Rockland man had fetched with him a she dog of marvelous craft and from her next litter he sent a pup to Chet. In honor of the giver Chet called the dog Job. And Job—Old Tantrybogus that was to be—learned that the farm upon the hill was his world and his home.

Chet's farm, numbering some eighty acres, included meadows that cut thirty or forty tons of hay; it included ample pasturage for a dozen cows; and it ran down to the George's River behind the barn, through a patch of hardwood growth that furnished Chet with firewood for the cutting—a farm fairly typical of Fraternity. No man might grow rich upon its fruits, but any man with a fair measure of industry could draw a pleasant living from it and find time for venturing along the brooks for trout or through the alder runs after woodcock or into the swamps for deer, according to the season. From the wall that bounds the orchard you may look down to where the little village lies along the river. A dozen or so of houses, each scrupulously neat and scrupulously painted; a white church with its white spire rising above the trees; the mill straddling the river just below the bridge, and a store or two. Will Bissell's store is just above the bridge, serving as market place and forum. The post office is there, and there after supper the year round Fraternity foregathers.

In Fraternity most men own dogs; not the cross-bred and worthless brutes characteristic of small towns in less favored countrysides, but setters of ancient stock or hounds used to the trail of fox or rabbit. Now and then you will see a collie or a pointer, though these breeds are rare. Utilitarian dogs—dogs which have tasks to do and know their tasks and do them.

Most men in Fraternity own or have owned some single wonderful dog of which they love to tell—a dog above all other dogs for them, a dog whose exploits they lovingly recount. And it was to come to pass that Job, better known as Old Tantrybogus, should be such a dog to Chet McAusland.

## II

Your true setter is born, not made. The instincts of his craft are a part of his birthright. Nevertheless they must be guided and cultivated and developed. There are men whose profession it is to train bird dogs, or as the phrase goes, to break them. With some of these men it is a breaking indeed, for they carry a lash into the field, nor spare to use it. Others work more gently to a better end. But any man may make his dog what he will if he have patience coupled with the gift of teaching the dog to understand his wishes.

Chet decided to train Job himself. He set about it when the pup was some six months old, at a season when winter was settling down upon the farm and there were idle hours on his hands. He had kept as trophies of the gunning season just past the head and the wings of a woodcock. These he bound into a ball of soft and woolly yarn and on a certain day he called Job to his knee and made him sniff and smell this ball until the puppy knew the scent of it. Job wished to tear and rend the pleasantly soft and yielding plaything, but Chet forbade this by stern word, backed by restraining hand, till the pup seemed to understand.

Then he looped about the dog's neck a stout cord and he held this cord in his hand, the pup at his feet, while he tossed the woolen ball across the kitchen floor. The pup turned and leaped after the ball.

Before he could make a second jump Chet said sharply, "Whoa!"

And he snubbed the cord he held so that Job was brought up short in a tumbling heap, his toe nails scratching on the floor.

Chet got up and crossed and picked up the ball; he returned to his chair, called the pup to his knee, tossed the ball again. Again Job darted after it and again Chet said, "Whoa," and checked Job with the cord. At which the puppy, with the utmost singleness of purpose, caught the cord in his mouth, squatted on the floor and set about gnawing his bonds in two. Chet laughed at him, called him in, fetched the ball, and tried again.

After Chet had checked him half a dozen times with voice and string the pup sat on its small haunches, looked at Chet with his head on one side and wrinkled its furry brow in thought. And Chet repeated slowly over and over:

"Whoa, Job! Whoa! Whoa!"

The lesson was not learned on the first day or the second or the third. But before the week was gone Job had learned this much: That when Chet said "Whoa" he must stop, or be stopped painfully. Being a creature of intelligence, Job thereafter stopped; and when he was sure the pup understood, Chet applauded him and fed him and made much of him.

One day in the middle of the second week, Job having checked at the word of command, Chet waited for a moment and then said, "Go on!"

Job looked round at Chet, and the man motioned with his hand and repeated, "Go on, Job!"

The pup a little doubtfully moved toward where lay the woolly ball. When he was within a yard of it Chet said again, "Whoa!"

When he stopped this time he did not look back at Chet but watched the ball, and Chet after a single glance threw back his head and laughed aloud and cried to himself, "Now ain't that comical?"

For Job, a six-months' puppy, was on his first point. Head low and flattened, nose on a line toward the ball, legs stiff, tail straight out behind with faintly drooping tip, the pup was motionless as a graven dog—a true setter in every line.

And Chet laughed aloud.

This laughter was a mistake, for at the sound the pup leaped forward, the cord slipped through Chet's fingers and the dog caught the woolly ball and began to worry it. Chet, still laughing, took the ball from him, caressed him, praised him and ended the lesson for that day. And by so doing he permitted the birth in Job of one fault which he would never be able to overcome. The pup supposed he had been applauded for capturing the woolly ball and that notion would never altogether die in his dog brain. Job would break shot, as the gunners say, till the end of his days.

## III

By October of his second year Job was sufficiently educated to be called a good working dog. He would stop at the word of command; he would swerve to right or left at a hand gesture; he would come to heel; he would point and hold his point as long as the bird would lie. He was a natural retriever, though Chet had to correct a tendency to chop the object that was retrieved. The man did this by thrusting through and through the woolen teaching ball a dozen long darning needles. When the dog, retrieving this ball, closed his jaws too harshly these needles pricked his tender mouth. He learned to lift the ball as lightly as a feather; he developed a mouth as soft as a woman's hand; and even in his second year he would at command retrieve an egg which Chet rolled across the kitchen floor and never chip the shell.

His one fault, his trick of breaking shot, was buttressed and built into the dog's very soul by an incident which occurred in his first year's hunting. He and Chet left the farmhouse one afternoon and started down through the fringe of woodland toward the river. It was near sunset. Chet had his gun, and as he expected, they found game; Chet had ample warning when he saw Job stiffen at half point, his tail twitching. He watched until the dog began to move forward with slow steps, and he said to himself, "He's roding a pa'tridge. I knew there'd be one here."

Job's head was high, evidence in itself that he had located partridge rather than woodcock. Chet skirted the fringe in the open land, studying the ground well ahead of the dog, alert for the burst of drumming wings. He moved quietly and Job moved among the trees, his feet stirring the leaves. The dog was tense; so was the man. And presently the dog froze again, this time in true point, tail rigid as an iron bar.

Chet knew that meant the partridge had squatted, would run no more. Forced to move now, the bird would fly. He waited for a long half minute, but the partridge waited also. So Chet, rather than walk in among the trees and spoil his chance for a shot, stooped to pick up a stone, intending to toss it in and frighten the bird to wing.

When he stooped, out of position to shoot, he heard the drum of pinions and saw rise not one partridge but two. They swept across the open below him, unbelievably swift, and Chet whipped up his gun and fired once and then again. And never a feather fell. The birds on set wings glided out of his sight into the edge of an evergreen growth down the hill where it would be hopeless to try for a shot at them again.

And Job pursued them. As the birds rose the dog had raced forward. As they disappeared among the tops of the low hemlocks the dog went out of sight after them. Ejecting the empty shells from his gun, Chet swore at himself for his poor shooting and swore at Job for breaking shot and loudly commanded the dog to return. Job did not do so; did not even respond when Chet put his whistle to his lips and blew. So the man started after the dog, whose bell he could faintly hear, and promised to find Job and teach him a thing he needed to know. He started toward the cover, whistling and shouting for Job to come to heel.

When he was half way across the open Job did emerge from the shelter of the evergreens, and he came toward Chet at a swift trot, head held high. Chet started to abuse him. And then when the dog was still half a dozen rods away he saw that Job carried a cock partridge in his mouth. The bird, wounded unto death, had flown to the last wing beat far into the wood. And Job pursuing had found the game and was fetching it in.

For consistency's sake and for the dog's sake Chet should still have punished Job—should still have made him understand that to break shot was iniquity. But Chet was human and much too warm-hearted to be a disciplinarian. Perhaps he is not to be blamed for praising Job after all. Certainly the man did praise the dog, so that Job's dog brain was given again to understand that if he chased a bird and caught it he would be applauded. The fault dwelt in him thereafter.

"I tried to break him all his life," Chet will say. "I put a rope on him and a choke collar and I shook him up—everything I knew. It wan't no good. But it was my fault in the beginning. I never really blamed Old Tantry—never could."

## IV

This is not properly the story of Job's youth or of his life, but of his aging and the death of him. Nevertheless there was much in his life that was worth the telling. His reputation rests not on Chet's word alone—the village knew him and was proud of him. His renown began in his third year in deep winter when Chet and Jim Saladine went fishing one day through the ice on Sebacook Pond. Chet and Saladine became separated, one on either side of the lower end of the pond, and Jim had the pail of bait. Chet made Job go after the pail clear across the pond and fetch it to him and take it back to Saladine again. The dog's sagacity and understanding, evidenced then and chronicled by Saladine at Bissell's store that night, were to wax thereafter for half a dozen years; and even when the dog grew old his understanding never waned.

It was in his ninth year that Job had his greatest day—a day into which he crowded epic deeds enough to make heroes of half a dozen dogs. And the tale of that day may perhaps be worth the telling.

Chet had taken Job out the night before to try for a partridge in the fringes of the wood below the farm. They were late in starting, but within fifteen minutes Job was marking game and just at sunset the bird rose and wheeled toward the thickets of the wood. Chet had a snap shot; he took it and he saw the bird's legs drop and dangle before it disappeared. He knew what that meant. A body wound, a deadly wound. The bird would fly so long as its wings would function, then set its pinions and glide in a long slant to earth, and when it struck ground it would be dead.

He sent Job into the wood, himself followed the dog, and he was in haste, for dark was already coming down. He hunted till he could no longer see—found nothing. In the end he called Job in, and the dog reluctantly abandoned the search at Chet's command and followed his master back to the farm.

Two Rockland men telephoned that evening asking if they might come to the farm next day and try for birds; and Chet, who can always find time for a day's gunning, bade them come. Doctor Gunther, who was telephoning, said: "Hayes and I'll be there by half past eight. Mind if we bring our dogs?"

"Mind? No," said Chet. "Sure!"

"They're wild," said the doctor, "but I'd like to have them work with Job—do them good."

"Best thing in the world for them," Chet agreed. "Let them back him on a few points and it'll steady them. I'll look for you."

In the morning he rose early and busied himself with his chores so that he might be ready when the hunters came. It was not an ideal hunting day. The morning was lowery and overcast and warm and there was a wind from the east that promised fog or rain. With an eye on the clouds Chet worked swiftly. He fed Job in the shed where the dog usually slept and it chanced that he left the door latched so that Job was a prisoner until the others arrived. They were a little ahead of time and Chet asked them to wait a little. He had been picking apples in the orchard behind the shed and he took them out there to see the full barrels of firm fruit. Job went out into the orchard with them and no one of the men noticed that the dog slipped away beyond the barn toward the woods.

When a little later they were ready to start Chet missed the dog. He is a profane man, and he swore and whistled and called. Hayes, the man who had come with Gunther, winked at the doctor and asked Chet: "Is he a self-hunter? Has he gone off on his own?"

"Never did before," Chet said hotly. His heat was for Job, not for Hayes. "I'll teach him something!"

He went out behind the barn, still whistling and calling, and the others followed him. Their dogs were in the car in which they had come from Rockland. The three men walked across the garden to the brow of the hill above the river and Chet blew his whistle till he was purple of countenance. The other two were secretly amused, as men are apt to be amused when they find that an idol has feet of clay. For Job was a famous dog.

Hayes it was who caught first sight of him and said, "There he comes now."

They all looked and saw Job loping heavily up the slope through an open fringe of birches. But it was not till he scrambled over the wall that they saw he bore something in his mouth.

Hayes said, "He's got a woodchuck."

Chet, with keener eyes, stared for a moment, then exclaimed exultantly: "He's got that partridge I killed down there last night! I knew that bird was dead."

They were still incredulous, even after he told them how he had shot the bird the night before.

They were incredulous until Job came near enough for them all to see, came trotting to Chet and proudly dropped the splendid bird at his master's feet. When they could no longer doubt they exclaimed. For such a feat is alone enough to found a dog reputation on.

As for Chet, though he was swelled with pride, he made light of the matter.

"You'll see him work to-day though," he said. "The scent lies on a day like this. But it'll rain by noon—we want to get started."

They did get started and without more delay. They went in the car, and after a mile or so stopped on a rocky ledge beside the road at what Chet was used to call the Dummy Cover—an expanse of half a dozen acres tangled with alders and birches and thorn and dotted with wild apple trees here and there. Two or three low knolls lifted their heads above the muck of the lower land—an ideal place for woodcock when the flight was on.

The men got out and belled their dogs and old Job stood quietly at Chet's heel while Chet filled his pockets with shells. The other dogs were racing and plunging, breaking across the wall, returning impatiently at command, racing away again. When they were ready the three men went through the bars, and with a gesture Chet sent Job into an alder run to the right. The great dog began his systematic zigzagging progress, designed to cover every foot of the ground, while the younger dogs circled and scuffled and darted about him, nosing here and there, wild with the excitement of the hunt.

Such dogs flush many birds and one of these dogs flushed a woodcock now fifty yards ahead of where old Job was working. The bird started to circle back, saw the men and veered away again. Though the range was never less than forty yards, Chet, who had a heavy far-shooting gun, took a snap shot through the alder tops as the bird turned in flight and he saw it jump slightly in the air as though the sound of the gun had startled it. Chet knew what that little break in its flight had meant and he watched the bird as long as he could see it and marked where it scaled to earth at last in the deeps of the cover ahead of them.

It was while his attention was thus distracted that Job disappeared. When Chet had reloaded he looked round for the dog and Job was gone. He listened and heard no sound of Job's bell. He blew his whistle and blew again. The other two dogs came galloping to their masters, heads up, eyes questioning, but Job did not appear.

The man Hayes said: "He's gone off alone. I wouldn't have a dog I couldn't keep in."

Chet looked at him with a flare of his native temper in his eyes.

"He's got a bird," said Chet. "He's right here somewhere and he's got a bird."

He turned and began to push his way into the alders and the other two men kept pace with him, one on either side. It was hard going; they could see only a little way. Now and then Chet whistled again, but for the most part they went quietly. Woodcock may not be found in open stubble like the obliging quail. You will come upon them singly or by twos in wet alder runs or upon birch-clad knolls or even in the shelter of a clump of evergreens—in thick cover almost always, where it is difficult for a man to shoot; and the bird must usually be killed before it has gone twenty yards in flight or it goes scot-free.

In such a cover as this the men were now hunting for Job; and at the end of fifteen minutes, in which they had worked back and forth and to and fro without discovering the dog, Hayes and the doctor were ready to give up.

"Call him in," Hayes told Chet. "Maybe we'll see the bird get up. We can't find him and we're wasting time."

Chet hesitated, then he said: "I'll shoot. Maybe that'll scare up the bird."

On the last word his gun roared and through its very echoes each of the three men heard the tinkle of a bell, and Chet, who was nearest, cried: "There he is! Careful! The bird's moving."

The dog was in the very center of the cover they had traversed—in a little depression where he chanced to be well hidden. They had passed within twenty feet of him, yet had he held his point. Hayes was the first to do homage.

"By gad," he cried, "that is some dog, McAusland!"

"You be ready to shoot," Chet retorted. "I'll walk up the bird."

They said they were ready; he moved in to one side of Job and the woodcock got up on whistling wings. Hayes' first shot knocked him down.

Job found another bird a little farther on and Chet killed it before it topped the alders. Then they approached the spot where he had marked down that first woodcock, the one which had been flushed by the too-rangy dogs. He called Job, pointed, said briefly: "Find dead bird, Job."

The dog went in, began to work. When the other men came up Chet said: "I think I hurt that first bird. He dropped in here. Job will find him."

"Let's send the other dogs in, too," Hayes suggested. "Mine hasn't learned retrieving yet."

Chet nodded and the other two dogs plunged into the cover to one side of Job and began to circle, loping noisily. Job looked toward them with an air of almost human disgust at such incompetency, then went on with his business of finding the bird.

The men, watching, saw then a curious thing: they saw old Job freeze in a point and as he did so the other dogs charged toward him. One, Gunther's, caught the scent ten feet away and froze. The other hesitated, then came on—and Job growled, a warning deadly growl. The other dog stopped still.

Chet exclaimed: "Now ain't that comical? Hear old Job tell him to freeze?"

Hayes nodded and the three stood for a moment, watching the motionless dogs, silent. Then the young dog stirred again and Job moved forward two paces and flattened his head so low it almost touched the ground and—growled again.

Chet laughed.

"All right, Job," he called. "Dead bird! Fetch it in!"

Job did not move, and Hayes said: "Maybe it's not dead."

"I'll walk in," Chet told him. "I won't shoot. You do the shooting."

They nodded and he began to work in through the alders toward where Job stood. The others waited in vantage points outside. Chet came abreast of Job and stopped. But the dog stood still, and this surprised Chet, for Job was accustomed to rush forward, flushing up the bird as soon as he knew that Chet was near at hand. So the man studied the ground ahead of Job's nose, trying to locate the bird; and he moved forward a step or two cautiously and at last began to beat to and fro, expecting every minute to hear the whistle of the woodcock's wings as it rose.

Nothing happened. The two younger dogs broke point with a careless air as though to say they had not been pointing at all; that they had merely been considering the matter. They began to move about in the alders. And at last Chet, half convinced that Job was on a false point, turned to his dog and said harshly: "There's nothing here, Job. Come out of it. Come along. Come in."

Job watched Chet, but did not move. His lower jaw was fairly resting on the ground, and Chet exclaimed impatiently and stooped and caught his collar to drag him away. When he did this he saw the bird—saw its spreading wing beneath Job's very jaw—and he reached down and lifted it, stone dead, from where it lay. Not till Chet had taken up the woodcock did Job stir, but when he saw it safe in his master's hand he shook himself, looked at the other dogs with a triumphant cock of his ears and turned and trotted on down the run.

They left that cover presently, put in an hour in the Fuller pasture, where a partridge and two woodcock fell to their guns, and then drove back to the farm. It was beginning to rain—the thick brush soaked them. Chet bade them come and have dinner at the farm and wait on the chance that the afternoon would see a clearing sky. So they had a dinner of Chet's cooking, and afterward they sat upon the side veranda watching the rain, smoking.

Chet McAusland is an extravagantly generous man. If you go fishing with him you take home both your fish and his own. He will not have it otherwise. Likewise if you go into the covers the birds are yours.

"Sho, I can get woodcock any time! You take them," he will say. "Go on now."

And it is so obvious that he is happier in giving than in keeping that he usually has his way.

After dinner he brought out the birds that had been killed in the morning and laid them on an empty chair beside him and began to tie their legs together so that they could be conveniently handled. Job was on the floor a yard away, apparently asleep. The men were talking. And Job growled.

Chet looked down, saw there were kittens about—there were always kittens at the farm—and reproved Job for growling at the kits. He was a little surprised, for Job usually paid no attention to them, even permitted them to eat from his plate. He said good-naturedly: "What are you doing, Job? Scaring that little kitten? Ain't you ashamed!"

Job was so far from being ashamed that he barked loudly and Chet bent to cuff him into silence. Then he saw and laughed aloud. "Now ain't that comical!" he demanded. "Look a-there!"

One of the kittens under Chet's very chair was laboring heavily, trying to drag away a woodcock that seemed twice as large as itself. The other men laughed; Chet rescued the woodcock; the kitten fled and Job beamed with satisfaction and slapped his tail upon the floor.

Hayes cried: "By gad, McAusland, that dog has sense! I'd like to buy him."

"You don't want to buy him. He's getting old. He won't be able to hunt much longer."

"Is he for sale?"

"Oh, you don't want him," Chet said uncomfortably. He hated to refuse any man anything.

"I'll give you three hundred for him," said Hayes.

Now three hundred dollars was as much cash as Chet was like to see in a year's time, but—Job was Job. He hesitated, not because the offer attracted him but because he did not wish to refuse Hayes. He hesitated, but in the end he said, "You don't want old Job."

Gunther touched Hayes' arm, caught his eye, shook his head; and Hayes forbore to push the matter. But he could not refrain from praising Job.

"I never saw as good a dog!" he declared.

"He is a good dog," Chet agreed. "He'll break shot, but that's his only out. He's staunch, he'll mind, he works close in and he's the best retriever in the County."

"You don't lose many birds with him," Hayes agreed.

"I can throw a pebble from here right over the barn and he'll fetch it in," said Chet. "There's nothing he won't bring—if I tell him to."

Gunther laughed.

"You're taking in a good deal of territory, Chet."

"I could tell you some things he's done that would surprise you," Chet declared.

Hayes chuckled.

"Let's try him out," he suggested.

"All right."

Hayes pointed toward the barn. The great doors were open and a yellow and black cat was coming through the barn toward them. As Hayes pointed her out she sat down in the doorway and began to lick her breast fur down.

"Have him fetch the cat," said Hayes.

Chet laughed. He stooped and touched the dog's head.

"Job," he said, "come here."

Job got up and stood at Chet's knee, looking up into his master's face, tail wagging slowly to and fro. Chet waved his hand toward the barn.

"Go fetch the cat," he said. "Go fetch the cat, Job." The dog looked toward the barn, looked up at Chet again. Chet repeated, "Fetch the cat, Job."

And the dog, a little doubtfully, left them and walked toward the barn. The cat saw Job coming, but was not afraid. They were old friends. All creatures were friends on Chet's farm. It rose as Job approached and rubbed against his legs. Job stood still, uncertain; he looked back at Chet, looked down at the cat, looked back at Chet.

"Fetch, Job!" Chet called.

Then the dog in a matter of fact way that delighted the three men on the porch closed his jaws over the cat's back, at the shoulder. The cat may have been astonished, but it is cat instinct to hang quietly when lifted in this wise. It made no more than a muffled protest; it hung in a furry ball, head drawn up, paws close against its body.

Job brought the cat gravely to Chet's knee, and Chet took it from his mouth and soothed it and applauded Job.

"I'll give you five hundred for that dog," said Hayes.

"You don't want to buy him," Chet replied slowly, and the two men saw that there was a fierce pride in his eyes.

## V

A dog does not live as long as a man and this natural law is the fount of many tears. If boy and puppy might grow to manhood and doghood together, and together grow old, and so in due course die, full many a heartache might be avoided. But the world is not so ordered, and dogs will die and men will weep for them so long as there are dogs and men.

A setter may live a dozen years—may live fifteen. Job lived fourteen years. But the years of his prime were only seven, less than his share, for in his sixth year he had distemper and hunted not at all then or the year thereafter. For months through his long convalescence he was too weak to walk and Chet used to go in the morning and lift the dog from his bed in the barn into a wheelbarrow; and he would wheel Job around into the sun where he might lie quietly the long day through. But in his eighth year he was himself again—and in his ninth and tenth he hunted.

When he was eleven years old his eyes failed him. The eye is the first target of old age in a setter. It fails while the nose is still keen. In August of Job's eleventh year he went into the fields with Chet one day when Chet was haying, and because the day was fine the dog was full of life, went at a gallop to and fro across the field.

Chet had begun to fear that Job was aging; he watched the dog now, somewhat reassured; and he said to Jim Saladine, who was helping him, "There's life in the old dog yet."

"Look at that!" said Saladine.

But Chet had seen. Job going full tilt across the field had run head-long into a bowlder as big as a barrel, which rose three feet above the stubble. He should have seen it clear across the field; he had not seen it at all. They heard his yelp of pain at the blow upon his tender nose and saw him get up and totter in aimless circles. Chet ran toward him, comforted him.

The dog was not stone blind, but his sight was almost gone. It must have gone suddenly, though Chet looking backward could see that he should have guessed before. Job was half stunned by the blow he had received and he followed Chet to the barn and lay down on a litter of hay there and seemed glad to rest. Chet, his eyes opened by what had happened, seemed to see the marks of age very plain upon the old dog of a sudden.

He took him into the covers that fall once or twice and Job's nose functioned as marvelously as ever. But Chet could not bear to see the old dog blundering here and there, colliding with every obstacle that offered itself. After the third trial he gave up and hunted no more that fall. He even refused to go out with others when they brought their dogs.

"My old Job can't hunt any more," he would say. "I don't seem to enjoy it any more myself. I guess I'll not go out to-day."

Hayes was one of those who tried to persuade Chet to take the field. An abiding friendship had grown up between these two. And late in October Hayes brought another puppy to the farm.

"He'll never be the dog Job was," he told Chet. "But he's a well-blooded dog."

"There won't ever be another Job," Chet agreed. "But—I'm obliged for the puppy—and he'll be company for Job."

He called the new dog Mac and he set about Mac's training that winter, but his heart was not in it. That Job should grow old made Chet feel his own years heavy upon him. He was still in middle life, as hale as any man of twenty. But—Job was growing old and Chet's heart was heavy.

Mary Thurman in the village—it was she whom Job called his mistress—saw the sorrow in Chet. She was full of sympathetic understanding of the man. They were as truly one as though they had been married these dozen years.

Annie Bissell, Will Bissell's wife, said to her once: "Why don't you marry him, Mary? Land knows, you've loved him long enough."

Mary Thurman told her: "He don't need me. He's always lived alone and been comfortable enough and never known the need of a woman. I'll marry no man that don't know he needs me and tells me so."

"Land knows, he needs someone to rid up that house of his. It's a mess," the other woman said.

"Chet don't need me," Mary insisted. "When he needs me I reckon I'll go to him."

She saw now the sorrow in Chet's eyes and she tried to talk him out of it and to some extent succeeded.

Chet laughed a little, rubbed Job's head, said slowly: "I hate to see the old dog get old, that's all."

"Sho," said Mary, "he's just beginning to enjoy living. Don't have to work any more."

In the end she did bring some measure of comfort to Chet. And it was she who christened Job anew. He and Chet came down one evening, stopped on their way for the mail, and she greeted Chet and to the dog said, "Hello, Old Tantrybogus."

Chet looked at her, asked what she meant.

"Nothing," Mary told him. "He just looks like an old tantrybogus, that's all."

"What is a tantrybogus?" Chet asked. "I don't believe there's any such thing."

"Well, if there was he'd look like one," said Mary.

The name took hold. Mary always used it; Chet himself took it up. By the time Job was twelve years old he was seldom called anything else.

Chet had expected that Mac, the young dog, would prove a companion for Job, but at first it seemed he would be disappointed. To begin with, Job was jealous; he sulked when Chet paid Mac attention and was a scornful spectator at Mac's training sessions. This early jealousy came to a head about the time Mac got his full stature—in a fight over a field mouse. It happened in the orchard, where Chet was piling hay round his trees. Mac dug the mouse out of the grass, Old Tantrybogus stole it and Mac went for him.

Tantry was old, but strength was still in him, and some measure of craft. He got a neck hold and it is probable he would have killed Mac then and there if Chet had not interfered. As it was, Chet broke the hold, punished both dogs and chained them up for days till by every language a dog can muster they promised him to behave themselves. They never fought again. Mac had for Tantry a deep respect; Job had for Mac—having established his ascendancy—a mild and elderly affection.

In Tantry's thirteenth year during the haying Mac caught a mouse one day and brought it and gave it to the older dog; and Chet, who saw the incident, slapped his knee and cried, "Now ain't that comical?"

About his twelfth year old Tantry's bark had begun to change. Little by little it lost the deeper notes of the years of his prime; it lost the certainty and decision which were always a part of the dog. It began to crack, as an old man's voice quavers and cracks. A shrill querulous note was born in it. Before he was thirteen his bark had an inhuman sound and Chet could hardly bear to hear it. On gunning days while Chet was preparing to take the field with Mac, Old Tantrybogus would dance unsteadily round him, barking this hoarse, shrill, delighted bark.

It was like seeing an old man gamboling; it was age aping youth. There was something pitiful in it, and Chet used to swear and chain Tantry to his kennel and bid him—abusively—be still.

The chain always silenced Tantry. He would lie in the kennel, head on his paws in the doorway, and watch Chet and Mac start away, with never a sound. And at night when they came home Chet would show him the birds and Tantry would snuffle at them eagerly, then hide his longing under a mask of condescension as though to say that woodcock had been of better quality in his day.

In his thirteenth year age overpowered Tantry. His coat by this time was long; it hung in fringes from his thin flanks, through which the arched ribs showed. His head drooped, his tail dragged; his long hair was clotted into tangles here and there, because he was grown too old to keep himself in order. The joints of his legs were weak and he was splayfooted, his feet spreading out like braces on either side of him. When he walked he weaved like a drunken man; when he ran he collided with anything from a fence post to the barn itself. His eyes were rheumy. And he was pathetically affectionate, pushing his nose along Chet's knee, smearing Chet's trousers with his long white hairs. In his prime he had been a proud dog, caring little for caresses. This senile craving for the touch of Chet's hand made Chet cry—and swear. It was at this time that Mary Thurman told Chet he ought to put Tantrybogus away.

"He's too old for his own good," she said—"half sick, and sore and uncomfortable. He ain't happy, Chet."

Chet told her that he would—some day. But the day did not come, and Mary knew it would not come. Nevertheless she urged Chet more than once to do the thing.

"You ought to. He'd be happier," she said—"and so would you. You ain't happy with him around."

Chet laughed at her.

"I guess Old Tantry won't bother me long as he wants to live," he said.

"He makes you feel like an old man, Chet McAusland, just to look at him," she protested. But Chet shook his head.

"I won't feel old long as I can see you," he told her.

So Old Tantry lived on and grew more decrepit. One day in the winter of his thirteenth year he followed Chet down into the wood lot and hunted him out there—and was so weary from his own exertions that Chet had to carry the dog up the hill and home and put him to bed in the barn.

"I ought to put you away, Tantry," he said to himself as he gave the weary old creature a plate of supper. "It's time you were going, old dog. But I can't—I can't."

His fourteenth year saw Tantrybogus dragging out a weary life. Till then there had been nothing the matter with him save old age, but in his fourteenth summer a lump appeared on his right side against the ribs, and it was as large as a nut before Chet one day discovered it. Thereafter it grew. And at times when the old dog lay down on that side he would yelp with pain and get up hurriedly and lie down on the other side. By September the lump was half as large as an apple. And when Chet touched it Tantry whined and licked Chet's hand in a pitiful appeal. Even then Chet would not do that which Mary wished him to do.

"He'll go away some day and I'll never see him again," he told her. "But as long as he wants to stay—he'll stay."

"It's cruel to the dog," Mary told him. "You keep him, but you won't let him do what he wants to do. I'm ashamed of you, Chet McAusland."

Chet laughed uncomfortably.

"I can't help it, Mary," he said.

## VI

October came—the month of birds, the month when a dog scents the air and feels a quickening in his blood and watches to see his master oil the gun and break out a box of shells and fetch down the bell from the attic. And on the third day of the season, a crisp day, frost upon the ground and the sun bright in the sky, Chet decided to go down toward the river and try to find a bird.

When the bell tinkled Mac came from the barn at a gallop and danced on tiptoe round his master so that Chet had difficulty in making him stand quietly for as long as it took to adjust the bell on his collar. Old Tantrybogus had been asleep in the barn, and he was as near deaf as he was blind by this time, so that he heard nothing. But the stir of

Mac's rush past him roused the old dog and he climbed unsteadily to his feet and came weaving like a drunken man to where Chet stood. And he barked his shrill, senile, pitiful bark and he tried in his poor old way to dance as Mac was dancing.

Chet looked down at the old dog and because there were tears in his eyes he spoke harshly.

"Tantry, you old fool," he said, "go lie down. You're not going. You couldn't walk from here to the woods. Go lie down and rest, Tantry."

Tantry paid not the least attention; he barked more shrilly than ever. He pretended that it was a matter of course that Chet would bell him and take him along. This is one of the favorite ruses of the dog—to pretend to be sure of the treat in store for him until his master must have a heart of iron to deny him.

Tantry continued to dance until Chet walked to the kennel and pointed in and said sternly, "Get in there, Tantry!"

Then and only then the old dog obeyed. He did not sulk; he went in with a certain dignity, and once inside he turned and lay with his head in the door, watching Chet and Mac prepare to go. Chet did not chain him. There was no need, he thought. Tantry could scarce walk at all, much less follow him to the fringe of woodland down the hill.

When he was ready he and Mac went through the barn and across the garden into the meadow and across this meadow and the wall beyond till the hill dropped steeply toward the river. Repeated commands kept Mac to heel, though the dog was fretting with impatience. Not till they were at the edge of the wood did Chet wave his hand and bid the dog go on.

"Now find a bird, Mac," Chet commanded. "Go find a bird."

And Mac responded, moving into the cover at a trot, nosing to and fro. They began to work along the fringe down toward the river, where in an alder run or two Chet hoped to find a woodcock. Neither of them looked back toward the farm and so it was that neither of them saw Old

Tantrybogus like a shadow of white slip through the barn and come lumbering unsteadily along their trail. That was a hard journey for Tantry. He was old and weak and he could not see and the lump upon his side was more painful than it had ever been before. He passed through the barn without mishap, for that was familiar ground. Between the barn and the garden he brushed an apple tree that his old eyes saw too late. In the garden he blundered among the dead tops of the carrots and turnips, which Chet had not yet harvested. He was traveling by scent alone, his nose to the ground, picking out Chet's footsteps. He had not been so far away from the farm for months; it was an adventure and a stiff one. The wall between the garden and the meadow seemed intolerably high and a rock rolled under him so that he fell painfully. The old dog only whimpered a little and tried again and passed the wall and started along Chet's trail across the meadow.

Midway of this open his strength failed him so that he fell forward and lay still for a considerable time, tongue out, panting heavily. But when he was rested he climbed to his feet again—it was a terrible effort, even this—and took up his progress.

The second wall, which inclosed Chet's pasture, was higher and there was a single strand of barbed wire atop it. Tantry failed twice in his effort to leap to the top of the unsteady rank of stones and after that he turned aside and moved along the wall looking for an easier passage. He came to a bowlder that helped him, scrambled to the top, cut his nose on the barbed wire, slid under it and half jumped, half fell to the ground. He was across the wall.

Even in the trembling elation of this victory the old dog's sagacity did not fail him. Another dog might have blundered down into the wood on a blind search for his master. Tantrybogus did not do this. He worked back along the wall until he picked up the trail, then followed it as painstakingly as before. He was increasingly weary, however, and more than once he stopped to rest. But always when a thin trickle of strength flowed back into his legs he rose and followed on.

Chet and Mac had found no partridges in the fringe of the woods, so at the river they turned to the right, pushed through some evergreens and came into a little alder run where woodcock were accustomed to nest and where Chet expected to find birds lying on this day. Almost at once Mac began to mark game, standing motionless for seconds on end, moving forward with care, making little side casts to and fro. Chet's attention was all on the dog; his gun was ready; he was alert for the whistle of the woodcock's wings, every nerve strung in readiness to fling up his gun and pull.

If Mac had not found game in this run, if Chet and the dog had kept up their swift hunter's gait, Old Tantrybogus would never have overtaken them, for the old dog's strength was almost utterly gone. But Chet halted for perhaps five minutes in the little run, following slowly as Mac worked uphill, and this halt gave Old Tantry time to come up with them. He lumbered out of the cover of the evergreens and saw Chet, and the old dog barked aloud with joy and scrambled and tottered to where Chet stood. He was so manifestly exhausted that Chet's eyes filled with frank tears—they flowed down his cheeks. He had not the heart to scold Tantry for breaking orders and following them.

He reached down and patted the grizzled old head and said huskily: "You damned old fool, Tantry! What are you doing down here?"

Tantry looked up at him and barked again and again and there was a rending ring of triumph in the old dog's cackling voice.

Chet said gently: "There now, be still. You'll scare the birds, Tantry. Behave yourself. Mac's got a bird here somewhere. Be still—you'll scare the birds."

For answer, as though his deaf old ears had caught the familiar word and read it as an order, Tantry shuffled past his master and worked in among the alders toward where Mac was casting slowly to and fro. Chet watched him for a minute through eyes so blurred he could hardly see and he brushed his tears away with the back of his hand.

"The poor old fool," he said. "Hell, let him have his fun!"

He took one step forward to follow the dogs—and stopped. For old Tantrybogus, a dog of dogs in his day, had proved that he was not yet too old to know his craft. Unerringly, where Mac had blundered for a minute or more, he had located the woodcock—he was on point. And Mac, turning, saw him and stiffened to back the other dog.

Tantrybogus' last point was not beautiful; it would have taken no prize in field trials. His splayfeet were spread, the better to support his body on his tottering legs. His tail drooped to the ground instead of being stiffened out behind. His head was on one side, cocked knowingly, and it was still as still. When Chet, frankly weeping, worked in behind him he saw that the old dog was trembling like a leaf and he knew this was no tremor of weakness but a shivering ecstasy of joy in finding game again.

Chet came up close behind Old Tantry and stopped and looked down at the dog. He paid no heed to Mac. Mac was young, unproved. But he and Tantry, they were old friends and tried; they knew each the other.

"You're happier now than you've been for a long time, Tantry," said Chet softly, as much to himself as to the dog. "Happy old boy! It's a shame to make you stay at home."

And of a sudden, without thought or plan but on the unconsidered impulse of the moment, Chet dropped his gun till the muzzle was just behind Old Tantry's head. At the roar of it a woodcock rose on shrilling wings—rose and flew swiftly up the run with never a charge of shot pursuing. Chet had not even seen it go.

The man was on his knees, cradling the old dog in his arms, crying out as though Tantry still could hear: "Tantry! Tantry! Why did I have to go and—I'm a murderer, Tantry! Plain murderer! That's what I am, old dog!"

He sat back on his heels, laid the white body down and folded his arms across his face as a boy does, weeping. In the still crisp air a sound seemed still ringing—the sound of a dog's bark—the bark of Old Tantrybogus, yet strangely different too. Stronger, richer, with a new and youthful timbre in its tones; like the bark of a young strong dog setting forth on an eternal hunt with a well-loved master through alder runs where woodcock were as thick as autumn leaves.

# VII

Half an hour after that Will Bissell chanced by Chet's farm and saw Chet fetching pick and shovel from the shed, and something in the other's bearing made him ask: "What's the matter, Chet? Something wrong?"

Chet looked at him slowly, said in a hoarse voice: "I've killed Old Tantrybogus. I'm going down to put him away."

And he went through the barn and left Will standing there, down into the wood to a spot where the partridges love to come in the late fall for feed, and made a bed there and lined it thick with boughs and so at last laid Old Tantry to sleep.

His supper that night was solitary and cheerless and dreary and alone. But—Will Bissell must have spread the news, for while Chet was washing the dishes someone knocked, and when he turned Mary Thurman opened the door and came in.

Chet could not bear to look at her. He turned awkwardly and sat down at the kitchen table and buried his head in his arms. And Mary, smiling though her eyes were wet, came toward him. There was the mother light in her eyes, the mother radiance in Mary Thurman's face. And she took Chet's lonely head in her arms.

"There, Chet, there!" she whispered softly. "I reckon you need me now."

## CHAPTER 11

# The Demon Dog of Deacon's Draw

By Jim Rikhoff

*My friend Jim Rikhoff has been a staple in my life and such a major figure in the outdoor communications arena for so long that I can't remember a time when he wasn't around. Public relations director of Winchester, founder of Amwell Press, author of a column in* American Rifleman *and of stories in magazines like* Outdoor Life, *Jim has had so many lives in his near-ninety years that keeping up with him makes me dizzy. His love of big game hunting is topped only by his love of gun dogs and bird hunting. Typical of that passion is this story from* American Rifleman. *Jim is still with us, and the Rikhoff torch is now also being carried by his son, a top producer at CBS Sports in golf, football, and big sport specials.*

## I

Munroe Gordon first saw Josiah Cartwright's pointer dog on one of those stark, piercingly cold nights that sometimes suddenly close out Indian summer.

One day it had been pleasantly warm, the leaves just beginning to turn and the air a little lazy. Then, without warning, the first frost swept in with a vengeance. Still and clear. Full moon and no wind. Just plain, old-fashioned cold. A sound could be heard for ten miles and it seemed a man could almost see as far by the light of that moon at midnight as he might during the day.

With the first hint of frost and the bite of clear cold on his face, the young man broke out his shotgun and fetched his ancient hound, Paddle Foot, for their traditional first coon hunt of the season. Paddle Foot would never win an award for grace and beauty, but what he lacked in looks, he made up for in cagy, old-fashioned experience well tempered with natural instinct and seasoned with courage. Paddle Foot also loved his young master as only a dog grown old in service to one man can. And the affection was returned in full by his owner. Gordon owned other dogs—a young setter he doted upon and a disreputable Labrador—but, as he often said, Paddle Foot had raised him from a whelp.

It was a good night for coon hunting and man and dog soon forgot the cold in the intensity of their pursuit. They had left home after a late supper and, the brisk air invigorating every step after they left their pick-up, soon found themselves deep into the woods by 10 p.m. They had had a good run with a young coon at the end of the line and both partners were pleased with their fine beginning.

Munroe Gordon was a pleasant, open-faced man in his early twenties. Although relatively young among the sages of an ancient sport, his hunting abilities and gentle talents with hunting dogs of all breeds had won him a respect among his peers far beyond his years.

They had wandered through the woods—driven by the drive of their first chase—into areas unfamiliar to the young hunter and even his companion hound. The woods were deep and dark—even for this moonlit night—and gave little evidence of ever having had much contact with man and his tools. The wind had quieted and with it the woods. The moon had drifted behind a transient cloud and the resultant darkness cast a strange sense of detached isolation on the forest. Munroe had stopped, listening for any sound to break the uneasy silence. And then an alien clatter and eerie howl cut through the air to fill their ears. Paddle Foot growled and then, strangely, whimpered by his master's side.

Munroe stood, unmoving and silent, listening to the rattle of stones and snapping of twigs. The noise grew louder and more insistent. He lifted his gun and wheeled to see a deer—his tongue and eyes protruding in exhaustion and fear—bounding through the open glade beside him. And then, lunging through the brush, eyes gleaming in the night and body steaming in the cold air, a huge dog—liver and white—pounded into view. A pale glow radiated from the dog's heaving muscled body. Swamp glow. Fox-fire. All the strange and eerie phenomena sometimes seen in unlikely places ran through Munroe's mind, but this unnatural iridescence defied comparison or explanation. As the great dog started across the clearing intense on his quarry, young Gordon released his breath in a long gasp.

The dog stopped, sniffing the air and casting his head in slow, methodic rhythm from side to side. Munroe stood frozen in the shadow of the trees. Then the dog stopped and stood looking in his direction, some twenty yards away and deadly still, his obscene coat casting its sickening light into the shadows about it. The man could hear the dog's steady panting. Suddenly he remembered his gun.

He couldn't raise him arms. The dog just stood there and stared at him, seemingly weighing something in his mind. And then Munroe heard a snarling, whining growl from beside him. Before he realized what Paddle Foot was doing, the old hound had charged the intruder.

The big dog made one swift movement, quick for so large a beast, and before Munroe's stunned eyes, Paddle Foot was stretched lifeless in the eternity of one moment. A man stepped from the woods behind the dog. He had made no sound, but Munroe Gordon—his mind deadened by the sudden murder of his dog—seemed unsurprised by the stranger's unexpected appearance.

He was a tall, dark wiry man with the blackest hair of any man Munroe had ever seen. But it was his eyes, riveted above a hawkish nose and suspended under one atrocious, unbroken eyebrow, that told the story. Someone once called a man's eyes "windows of the soul." Well, he never met Josiah Cartwright. If he'd have looked in his eyes, he would have plumbed the depths of hell itself.

"Beezy," Josiah's voice quietly drifted through the air. With a contemptuous toss of his large gargoyle-like head, the dog reluctantly turned and trotted back toward the man. The man whispered something beyond the reach of the other man's ear and slipped into the darkness of the woods. The unworldly glow had disappeared and was lost in the night. The man turned to follow.

"Wait a minute, Mister," Munroe Gordon had found his voice as the dog departed, "What about my dog? Your dog killed my hound!" The man turned once more and looked at the young man standing before him. Munroe returned his stare, both men fixing each other's faces in their memories. The man stepped back into the shadows without a word and was gone. The younger man looked down at the stiffening flesh that had been his dog and made no move to follow. He had not recognized man or dog, but he would never forget either. He would meet them sooner than any of them would imagine.

## II

Josiah Cartwright had no wife or kin that acknowledged him and no man called him friend. He frightened children and made grown men strangely uneasy. It had always been so and, it appeared, with good cause. Josiah lived in a forgotten area of this world, the southern "Pine Barrens" of New Jersey. South Jersey—at least the interior—is a mysterious, unknown land to those who speed through the state by turnpike and expressway. Josiah's village—his was the only shack left standing with all four walls and roof—was a ghost town called Deacon's Draw. An itinerant, philandering preacher had been hung, drawn and quartered there in the 1700s as an example to other gentlemen of the cloth of similar persuasions.

Josiah's people—the inland "Pineys"—are a curious, inbred breed, increasingly suspicious and clannish with each generation. Some say these strange people—the ones we never see—are descended from Tory "cowboys" (guerillas we'd call them now) who fled to the Barrens after the Revolutionary War and later intermarried with the remaining Indians, runaway slaves, smugglers and lord-knows-what. It is not the sort of heritage that makes for good neighbors.

It's a poor district and the people poorer. Josiah and his kind had little to call their own—scant material wealth, the barest sort of existence, a limited future. It is a hard life with little recreation as the modern world knows it. The pleasure they receive from life is based on what's at hand—drinking, wenching, brawling, fishing, trapping and, most importantly, hunting.

Hunting is important to them: they can combine business with pleasure. Game laws mean little or nothing and a good many venison steaks have landed in New York restaurants by grace of a Piney's well-placed midnight shot. As with any business, the tools of the trade are valued most highly by the people who practice the trade. A good gun—and a good dog—are valuable, cherished possessions.

Josiah cared for nothing or no one in this world—except one thing, his large liver and white pointer. They were inseparable and people said they were well matched to deserve each other. The dog was as mean—if not meaner—than its master. But even Josiah's worst enemies had to admit that the dog was almost unbelievably uncanny on game. Josiah called his dog "Beelzebub's Demonly Delight" or just plain "Beezy" for short. Only when Josiah crooned "Beezy" as the dog egg-walked into a point, it almost sounded obscene.

No one knew where Josiah had found his pointer; everyone—at least in the Barrens—knew that Beezy was probably the best bird dog they had even seen. The "Pineys" were lucky in one respect: they had quail and they knew how to hunt quail dogs. Strangely enough, Josiah Cartwright had never before boasted a bird dog that even touched some of the fine pointers and setters fielded by his neighbors. That is, until Beezy hove up on the horizon one Fall night.

On that night a few of the Pineys happened by Josiah's shack—they were on their way to check a deadfall—and a large liver and white pointer came bounding out from behind the shed. He was a giant of a dog with a growl to match and even they, familiar as they were with all sorts of maverick dogs, were prudent enough to hesitate. They stood stock still while Beezy gave them a cold once-over. Josiah never volunteered any information concerning his arm or Beezy's background and people gave up asking, but not wondering.

Since it was Fall, it wasn't very long until Beezy's other talents became apparent. Hunters would occasionally run across Josiah and his dog in the field—after all, everyone knows the same quail coverts in a small locality—and it must be confessed that most times they abdicated the field to that formidable pair. Josiah had never been a creature to command undying affection; in company with Beezy, he was downright fearsome. But some of the retreating hunters watched after they withdrew to the shadows and what they saw livened up many a tale around Clurgy's Franklin stove.

Beezy was some quail dog—or, for that matter, grouse, woodcock and pheasant dog as well. People reported they saw Beezy plunge into frozen, ice-topped ponds after fallen ducks with no concern whatever for ice or chilling water. There he'd be, chopping through the thin-skinned ice like some primitive ice-breaker, water splashing all about and bearing down in relentless fashion on some hapless duck. Josiah didn't lose any cripples that year.

But Josiah Cartwright had long coveted some sort of stature that would set him apart (in a favorable light, that is) from other men.

Something that no man could take away. He knew he would never be rich or powerful, a captain of industry or respected leader of anything for that matter. But he could win the Sneaky Hollow field trial and for him that was more than enough.

## III

The Sneaky Hollow Invitational was a rare trial; entries were strictly limited to handlers and dogs native to the state. As such, it wasn't prey to the big professional trainers from the South and their large stables of rich men's dogs.

As a consequence, this "purified" trial had come to mean a lot to the state's amateur dog handlers. If a man could place at Sneaky Hollow, he had arrived at the senior rank among his peers in the tight circle of New Jersey's sporting dog world. If he—glory of glories—should happen to win, his life was complete. There could be little treasure left in this world for him; everything else would be anticlimactic in his remaining years.

The great day arrived and representatives of all sections of the state joined for the one event that brought them together in single-minded purpose each year. Tall, sandy Scotch-Irish from the hills of the northern part of the state joined the dark, smaller—and merrier— Italian-Americans of the flatlands of middle Jersey. A Hungarian refugee freedom fighter, accompanied by his aristocratic Vizsla pointer, from New Brunswick, rubbed elbows with a distinguished Anglo-Saxon, High Episcopalian doctor from Short Hills who, paradoxically, was accompanied by a rather nondescript, sturdy Brittany. Farmer, lawyer, businessman and commuter to New York, clergy and scoundrel, they were all united in one cause: sporting dogs.

And among them all—standing out like a foreign intrusion although they were perhaps of the oldest stock in the state—were the Pineys, the strange people of the southern Barrens. Awkward, withdrawn, shyly and slyly observing the goings-on with veiled eyes that darted behind their guarded eyelids, these men and their occasional woman stood apart although they were surrounded by the crowd. And, alone, even among his own, Josiah Cartwright and his great dog stood to one side under a great elm tree. They were biding their time.

A flurry of commotion stirred the crowd on one side and Josiah turned to see a handsome young man step out with a slim, racy setter by his side. The murmurs of the onlookers gave ample evidence of their esteem for both man and dog. It was Munroe Gordon and his young setter bitch, the "Jersey Belle," his standard-bearer in this year's invitational. Since young Gordon was no slouch when it came to either field trials or a little judicious betting on the side, the smart money was fast drifting to the Jersey Belle, popularly known as Belle.

Although she was young and dainty, as her name might imply, she had already established an impressive record as both a shooting dog and a winner of local field trials. She was a pretty little thing—all white with a light ticking of orange sprinkled across her muzzle and down her sides plus one orange ear—and Gordon doted on her as an older man might his mistress.

Josiah and Beezy sidled up behind Munroe and Belle as they registered. Beezy appraised the young setter with a malevolent eye, bared his teeth and growled a deep, menacing snarl in his throat. Belle lazily tossed her ears as though to rid of an itinerant flea or other loathsome object and turned away. Beezy made a lunge forward, but Josiah checked him with a yank of his lead. Munroe turned and surveyed the situation with a startled eye. He started forward, hesitated, then with his face a mask, quietly spoke.

"That's quite a pointer you've got there. I hope he's under control," he said.

"Control enough," Josiah grunted, his eyes veiled.

"He's a registered dog, I take it?" the young man questioned.

"Yes," Josiah said with a strange smile, "but not in your book—or any other you've seen!" Munroe stood looking at the pair for a second or two and then walked away with Belle at heel. Josiah turned and signed Beezy up for the Invitational.

The puppy stakes finished well before noon. The first heats of the Invitational were run as soon as the judges had finished a short snack. Being dedicated men—and also anxious to return home sometime before midnight—the judges ran the trial straight through the day with no formal midday break for lunch.

As a result, there was a constant flow of spectators and participants between the parking areas, the grandstands and the gallery as it followed the various heats on the courses outlined. More people arrived; some drifted away. Eighteen dogs were entered for a total of nine heats, averaging thirty minutes per heat. Anyway one viewed it, it was going to be a good afternoon's work.

Although the Invitational was limited to dogs native to the state, the entries were all of first-class caliber. It was apparent from the first heats that this was going to be one of the most strenuously contested competitions in the history of the event. In the third heat, Beezy and Josiah quickly established a standard that most dogs would find hard to equal.

Old "Beelzebub's Demonly Delight" was—as his name might suggest—literally hell-on-wheels when it came to bird work. His bracemate in the third heat, one "Kentucky Sky Lou," had been regarded by many as an up and coming pointer. After Beezy got through with her, she was lucky to get a ride home. There was no doubt, Beezy was the dog to beat. As the saying goes, a miss is as good as a mile—and nobody, least of all Munroe Gordon, cared anything about coming in second. If you couldn't beat Beezy, you were done.

Entry after entry, setter and pointer, Brittany and shorthair, sallied forth to do his best against the awesome performance Beezy had established early in the day. A pall hung over the assembled handlers as heat after heat was completed with the hateful downstate dog still triumphant. Resignation and then despair gripped the steadily dwindling group of waiting handlers as champion dog after champion dog was ground up by Beezy's standard set in the third heat. Try as they might, the dogs couldn't measure up.

While there is usually considerable argument about even the most trifling judicial field trial decision, no one could find even the lamest excuse to question Beezy's leadership. Through it all, Munroe Gordon remained unperturbed. Sprawled in nonchalant fashion against a station wagon, he regarded the pathetic fatalists about him with contempt and amusement. The Jersey Belle was entered in the eighth heat, which was soon to start.

Well, the eighth heat was Belle's all the way. "Fancy Dan's Bo" was Belle's bracemate and it must be admitted that "Bo" was game to the last. Bo refused to acknowledge what was obvious to everyone else, canine and human. He turned in an admirable performance, but the Jersey Belle, under the gentle guiding spirit of her master, capped her already winning heat with a beautiful closing point and double retrieve at the end of the course. One of the missed birds downed one with each barrel of his Winchester double gun. It was, so to speak, the frosting on the cake.

After a moment's consultation, the judges stepped forward and their leader announced that due to Belle's superlative performance and Beezy's already established position, there would be a runoff heat between those two dogs to decide the champion of the Invitational. The gallery went wild. It appeared that the downstate demon might be vanquished by a little faith, hope and charity after all.

The remaining heat of what was now officially the first series of the Invitational was run without incident. No other dog matched the winning performances put up by Beezy and Belle and even the handlers involved seemed anxious for the runoff heat to be started. They didn't have long to wait.

Never have right and wrong, black and white, good and evil appeared so sharply delineated, especially between dogs. No one ever thinks of a dog as evil, black-hearted or wicked, but Beezy seemed all of those things to the spectators of Sneaky Hollow. Beezy was too methodical in his hunting. He didn't really enjoy it for its own sake, but rather for some fiendish satisfaction. That was it. Beezy was too perfect for a dog. He had no apparent faults; he made humans uneasy. A dog shouldn't be superior to man—who has many faults and knows it. You couldn't really "like" Beezy. Nothing worse could be said about a dog.

"Gentlemen, prepare for the breakaway. Marshall, see to the gallery," one of the judges motioned to the crowd behind him. It was the largest number of spectators the field trails had witnessed in years. "All right. Mr. Cartwright, Mr. Gordon, you may commence."

Belle and Beezy lit out in parallel bursts. Quickly extinguished their initial nervous energy and settled down to business within seconds after release. Both interpreted the wind, cast accordingly and moved down field with the handlers and judges following, trailed by the gallery.

Beezy performed in his usual, cool, determined, seemingly perfect fashion, but Belle was a dog possessed—not by the devil for that was Beezy's domain—but by all the varied and talented ancestors that made up her bloodline. All her Laverack and Llewellin forebears must have showered their benevolent magic upon her nose and brain that day. Each forceful stride seemed to proclaim her joy in hunting; each carefully executed approach on game underlined her skillfully tutored training. If Beezy was a demonic machine, Belle was heavenly inspiration.

Beezy seemed to sense that things were different. For the first time, he had a serious challenger. His huge, powerful body tensed and he lunged forward with more determined force than he had before exhibited. But what Beezy supplied in sheer force and power, Belle made up in skill and tactics.

While Beezy covered ground in huge leaping bounds, determined to move through as much as territory as possible as fast as he could with the hope of finding the most birds, Belle picked her way with care in a steady, calculated lope. Finally it happened; Belle picked up a bird that Beezy—impatient in his determination—had missed. In fact, as the gallery murmured, Beezy had practically walked right over the bird. Josiah's face darkened with rage; Munroe's demeanor imparted nothing but a sort of serene calm.

"That's one for old Paddle Foot," he murmured.

Belle continued on her way. She never hesitated nor doubted what her instinct told her and her training dictated. Faultlessly moving through each course, the small white and orange-ticked setter picked her way from bird to bird with a sublime economy of movement. Beezy on his part became almost frantic with frustration and, it appeared, rage. It seemed as if he knew that he was losing out and it was more than he could bear. He became careless. Eager to even the score, Beezy pushed too hard on a running bird and it flushed wild ahead of him. The gallery roared. It was all over but the handing out of trophies.

The gallery had already started back to the starting point when a snarl—then a yelping cry of pain—froze them in their tracks. They turned to see Munroe rushing forward with unbelievable speed toward two struggling dogs. Beezy's huge head was fixed over Belle's, his jaws firmly, wrenchingly tearing at the slim neck of the setter. Blood coursed down the soft, white-feathered hair. Munroe Gordon raised a fist and slammed it against Beezy's head. Beezy, stunned, released his hold, staggered a moment and, shaking his head, turned on Munroe with bloody fangs. Josiah ran forward.

"Hold on, you devil! Hold on!" he shouted. Beezy stood there—his sides heaving, eyes dilated in flashing rage and madness, his mouth dripping saliva and blood.

"Get that dog out of here before I kill him. Right now! Get! And I swear I'll kill him if I ever see him again—anywhere." The younger man was breathing in slow controlled gasps. He had knelt by the Jersey Belle, who lay there, her quiet form occasionally jerking in spasmodic reaction to the shock of Beezy's brutal attack. Munroe had cleared the blood away from her neck. It appeared painfully, but not damagingly, torn. She would be well in a day or two, but it would be a long time before she—or anyone—forgot Beelzebub's Demonly Delight.

Josiah turned without a word. He walked away, up the road toward the woods, with Beezy at his heel. The judges, handlers and spectators remained silent as they watched the two leave. Josiah was the last Piney to leave. The rest—without sign or notice—had silently faded away during the first moments following Beezy's attack. Munroe Gordon straightened up and looked toward the retreating figures of Josiah and his dog. They were just cresting the hill. Without a word, Gordon—as if on some sort of premonition—started forward and, to the amazement of everyone, hastily trotted up the road to the top of the hill.

When he looked down, he saw Josiah—with Beezy at his left heel—pass down the other side of the hill until they were out of sight of the assembled crowd back at the grounds. Then Beezy stopped and seemingly with a low growl halted Josiah Cartwright. Josiah quickly turned and faced the dog. They remained motionless for a moment or two, some deadly silent struggle coursing over heaven knows what line of communication between them. Josiah seemed almost defiant in his stance; Beezy threatening.

Finally, Beezy gave a sharp, demanding snarl and impatiently tossed his head. Josiah's shoulders seemed to sag and with slow, agonized steps he walked back to the dog. The dog started forward, intent on its path; the man took a position at the dog's left heel and stumbled after him. It was almost dusk and Munroe Gordon was suddenly witness to a strange transition. As the sun's light faded in steady measure and the man's figure slowly blended into the shadows below, an eerie, almost phosphorescent light grew in contrasting proportion about the figure of the dog. And then . . . the little haze of light growing steadily brighter but ever smaller as it moved into the darkening distance—it simply disappeared.

It was the last sight anyone—in or out of those isolated Pine Barrens—ever had of Josiah Cartwright of Deacon's Draw and his dog, Beelzebub's Demonly Delight, who was sometimes called Beezy by his master.

## CHAPTER 12

# Mine Enemy's Dog

### By Ben Ames Williams

*This is our second excerpt from Ben Ames Williams' book* Thrifty Stock *(1923). In old New England hunters loved sitting around a hot stove and telling stories. Often their tales stretched the imagination to impossible limits. Sometimes the story was real, without the blemishes of tall tales. When the subject was bird dog training and performance in the field, things got downright serious, and the wrong words at the wrong time could turn good friends against one another. Here Williams shows us how that sometimes happened.*

# I

Fraternity has not changed in a hundred years; yet is there always some new thing in Fraternity. It may be only that Lee Motley's sow has killed her pigs, or that choleric Old Man Varney has larruped his thirty-year-old son with an ax helve, or that Jean Bubier has bought six yearling steers. But there is always some word of news, for the nightly interchange in Will Bissell's store, before the stage comes in with the mail. You may see the men gather there, a little after milking time, coming from the clean, white houses that are strung like beads along the five roads which lead into the village. A muscular, competent lot of men in their comfortable, homely garments. And they sit about the stove, and talk, and smoke, and spit, and laugh at the tales that are told.

Fraternity lies in a country of little towns and villages, with curious names something more than a century old. Liberty is west of Fraternity, Union is to the southward, Freedom lies northwest. Well enough named, these villages, too. Life in them flows easily; there is no great striving after more things than one man can use. The men are content to get their gardening quickly done so that they may trail the brooks for trout; they hurry with their winter's wood to find free time for woodcock and partridge; and when the snow lies, they go into the woods with trap for mink or hound for fox.

Thirty years ago there were farms around Fraternity, and the land was clear; but young men have gone, and old men have died, and the birches and the alders and the pines have taken back the land. There are moose and deer in the swamps, and a wildcat or two, and up in Freedom a man killed a bear a year ago. . . .

The hills brood over these villages, blue and deeper blue from range to farther range. There is a bold loveliness about the land. The forests, blotched darkly with evergreens, or lightly splattered with the gay tops of the birches, clothe the ridges in garments of somber beauty. Toward sunset a man may stand upon these hilltops and look westward into the purple of the hills and the crimson of the sky until his eyes are drunk with looking. Or in the dark shadows down along the river he may listen to the trembling silences until he hears his pulses pound. And now and then, with a sense of unreality, you will come upon a deer along some old wood road; or a rabbit will fluster from some bush and rise on haunches, twenty yards away.

The talk in Will Bissell's store turns, night by night, upon these creatures of the woods that lie about the town; and by the same token the talk is filled with speech concerning dogs. The cult of the dog is strong in Fraternity. Every man has one dog, some have two. These, you will understand, are real dogs. No mongrels here; no sneaking, hungry, yapping curs. Predominant, the English setter, gentlest and kindest and best-natured of all breeds; and, in second place, the lop-eared hounds. A rabbit hound here and there; but not many of these. Foxhounds more often. Awkward, low-bodied, heavy dogs that will nevertheless nose out a fox and push him hard for mile on mile. These are not such fox-hounds as run in packs for the sport of red-coated men. These are utilitarian dogs; their function is to keep the fox moving until the hunter can post himself for a shot. A fox skin is worth money; and cash money is scarce in Fraternity, as in all such little towns, and very hard to come by.

There are few sheep in Fraternity, so the dogs are free of that temptation; but there are deer. The deer is sacrosanct, to be taken only with rifle and ball, and by a woodcraft that bests the wild thing at its own game. No dog may justly chase a deer; and a dog so pursuing is outlawed and may legally be shot by any man. Men without conscience and dogs without honor will thus pursue the deer, in season and out; nevertheless, deer running is for the dogs of Fraternity the black and shameful crime.

They were talking dogs, on a certain night in late September, in Will Bissell's store. A dozen men were there; most of them from the village itself, two or three from outlying farms. Jim and Bert Saladine, both keen hunters of the deer, who killed their legal quota year by year, leaned side by side against the candy counter, and Andy Wattles sold them licorice sticks. Lee Motley had driven down from his farm above the Whitcher Swamp; and Jean Bubier had come in from the head of the Pond; and there was Gay Hunt; and there was George Freeland, and two or three besides. Proutt was one of these others, Proutt of South Fraternity, a farmer, a fox hunter, and a trainer of setter dogs. Finally, Nick Westley, a North Fraternity man, appointed within six months' time to be game warden for the district; a gentle man, well liked in spite of his thankless job; a man with a sense of humor, a steady and persistent courage, and a kindly tongue.

This night, as it happened, was to be the beginning of the enmity between Proutt and Westley. One-sided at first, this ill feeling. Two-sided at the last, and bitter enough on either side. A strange thing, dramatic enough in its development, fit to be numbered among the old men's tales that were told around the stove. . . .

Proutt, the dog breaker, was a man who knew dogs. None denied him that. "Yes," they would say; "Proutt'll break a dog for you. And when he gits done with your dog, your dog'll mind." If you scented some reservation in word or tone, and asked a question, you got no explanation. But your informant might say casually: "Hepperton's a good man with a dog, too. Over in Liberty. Gentles 'em."

Persistent inquiry might have brought out the fact that Hepperton never whipped a dog; that Proutt knew no other method. Lee Motley, who loved dogs, used to tell an incident. "Went out with Proutt once," he would explain. "After woodcock, we was. He was breaking a two-year-old. Nice a dog as I ever see. First bird, she took a nice point; but she broke shot. He had him a rawhide strap; and he called her in and I never see a dog hurt worse. And after that he, couldn't get her out from under his legs. Ain't been out with him since. Not me."

Proutt was not liked. He was a morose man, and severe, and known to nurse a grudge. But he turned out dogs which knew their business, and none denied him this. So had he his measure of respect; and his neighbors minded their own affairs and kept out of the man's harsh path.

Curiously enough, though he trained setters, Proutt did not like them. He preferred the hound; and his own dog—a lop-eared brown-and-white named Dan—was his particular pride. This pride was like the pride of a new father; it showed itself in much talk of Dan's deeds and Dan's virtues, so that Fraternity's ears were wearied with the name of Dan, and it was the fashion to grin in one's sleeve at Proutt's tales and to discredit them.

Proutt spoke, this night, of a day's hunting of the winter before. How, coursing the woods, he had heard a hound's bay far below him, and had taken post upon a ledge across which he thought the fox would come. "Dan 'uz with me," he said, in his hoarse loud voice. "I says to Dan: 'Set' and he set on his ha'nches, right aside me, cocking his nose down where t'other dog was baying, waiting, wise as an owl.

"I had my old gun, with Number Threes in both bar'ls; and me and Dan stayed there, awaiting; and the baying come nearer all the time, till I see the fox would come acrost that ledge, sure.

"Cold it was. Wind ablowing, and the snow acutting past my ears. Not much snow on the ground; but it was froze hard as sand. I figured Dan'd get uneasy; but he never stirred. Set where I'd told him to set; and us awaiting.

"Time come, I see the fox, sneaking up the ledge at that long, easy lope o' theirs. Dan see him too. His ears lifted and he looked my way. I says: 'Set.' And he let his ears down again, and stayed still. Fox come along, 'bout five rods below us. Crossed over there. So fur away I knowed I couldn't drop him. Never pulled; and he never saw me; and old Dan set where he was. Never moved a mite.

"After a spell, Will Belter's hound come past; and then come Will himself, cutting down from where he'd been waiting. Says: 'See a fox go by?' And I told him I did. He ast why I didn't shoot; and I says the fox was too fur off. And he says: 'Where was your dog?' So I told him Dan was setting right by me."

Proutt laughed harshly, and slapped a triumphant hand upon his knee. "Will wouldn't believe me," he declared, "till I showed him tracks, where he wuz, and where the fox went by."

He looked around for their admiration; but no one spoke at all. Only one or two glanced sidewise at each other, and slowly grinned. The tale was all right, except for a thing or two. In the first place, Proutt was no man to let a fox go by, no matter how long the shot; and, in the second place, Dan was known to be a surly dog, not overly obedient, unruly as his master. And, in the third place, this incident, thoroughly authenticated, had happened two years before to another man and another dog, as everyone in the store knew. Proutt had borrowed his tale from a source too close home. . . .

So they knew he lied; but no one cared to tell him so. Only, after a little silence, Nick Westley, the game warden, said with a slow twinkle in his eye: "Proutt, that reminds me of a story my father used to tell."

Proutt grunted something or other, disgusted with their lack of appreciation; and Westley took it for encouragement, and began to whittle slow, fine shavings from a sliver of pine which he held in hand, and told the tale.

"It was when he was younger," he explained, "before he was married, while he still lived at home. But I've heard him tell the story many a time.

"My Uncle Jim was living then; and he and my father had a hound. Good dog he was, too. Good as Dan, I think, Proutt.

"Well, one winter morning, with six or eight inches of loose snow on the ground, they were working up some old wood in the shed; and they saw the old hound drift off into the pasture and up the hill. And after a spell they heard him yelling down by the river.

Jim said to my father: 'He's got a fox.' And father said: 'Jim, let's go get that fox.' So they dropped their axes, and went in and got their guns, and they worked up through the pasture and over the hill till they located the dog's noise, and they figured the fox would come up around the hill by a certain way; and so they posted themselves there, one on either side of the path they thought he would take. And set to waiting. And it was cold as could be, and cold waiting, and they stamped their feet a little, but they couldn't move much for fear the fox would see them.

"So they were both well pleased when they saw the fox coming; and they both shot when he came in range, because they were cold and in a hurry and anxious to be done.

"Well, they shot into each other. Jim yelled: 'Damn it, my legs are full of shot!' And my father said: 'Mine too, you clumsy coot!' So they made remarks to each other for a spell; and then Jim said: 'Well, anyway, there's the fox; and I'm full of your shot, and I'm half froze. Let's skin the darn critter and get home.'

"So father agreed; and they went at it. The old dog had come up by then, and was sitting there with an eye on the fox, as a dog will. And father took the front legs and Jim took the hind legs, and they worked fast. And they kept cussing their hurts, and the cold, and each other. But they slit the legs down, and skinned out the tail, and trimmed up the ears and all, knives flying. And when they got about done, Jim, he said:

"'Look ahere, there's not a bullet in this fox.'

"Well, they looked, and they couldn't find a hole. Only there was a blue streak across the fox's head where a bullet had gone. And that was queer enough, but father said: 'I don't give a hoot. There's bullets enough in me. Skin out his nose and let's go.'

"So they cussed each other some more, and finished it up; and Jim, he heaved the carcass out into the brush, and father slung the skin over his shoulder, and they turned around to start home.

"Well, just about then the old dog let out behind them, and they whirled around. And father always used to say that, mad as they were at each other, they forgot all about it then; and they bust out laughing. He said you couldn't blame them. He said you never saw anything funnier.

"You see, that fox was just stunned. The cold snow must have revived him. Because when my father and Uncle Jim looked around, that skinless fox was going up over the hill like a cat up a tree—and the old dog hot on his heels."

The store rocked with their mirth as Westley stopped. Lee Motley roared, and the Saladines laughed in their silent fashion, and Will Bissell chuckled discreetly behind Proutt's back. Westley himself displayed such surprise at their mirth that they laughed the more; and fat little Jean Bubier shook a finger at Proutt and cried:

"And that will put the bee to your Dan, M'sieu Proutt. That will hold your Dan for one leetle while, I t'ink."

Proutt himself was brick-red with fury; and his eyes were black on Westley; but he pulled himself together, and he laughed . . . shortly.

His eyes did not leave Westley's face. And Lee Motley found a chance to warn the warden a little later. "It was a good joke," he said. "You handed it to him right. But look out for the man, Westley. He's mad."

Westley, still smiling, was nevertheless faintly troubled. "I'm sorry," he said. "I did it for a joke."

"He can't take a joke," said Motley.

The warden nodded, considering. "I'll tell you," he told Motley. "I'll square it with him."

"If it was me," Motley agreed, "I would."

Westley did not like to make enemies. And there had been only the friendliest malice in his jest. He took his measures to soothe Proutt before they left the store that night.

Westley had a dog, a setter, clean-blooded, from one of the country's finest kennels. A New York man who had shot woodcock with the warden the year before had sent the dog as a friendly gift, and Westley accepted it in the same spirit. In its second year and still untrained, it had nevertheless won Westley and won his wife and his children. They all loved the dog, as they loved each other. . . .

Originally this dog had been called Rex. The Westleys changed this name to Reck, which may be short for Reckless, or may be a name by itself. At any rate, it pleased them, and it pleased the dog. . . .

The dog was untrained, and Westley had no time for the arduous work of training. He had meant to send Reck, this fall, to Hepperton, in Liberty; but, to make his amends to Proutt, he took the latter aside this night and asked Proutt to take the training of the dog.

On longer consideration, he might not have done this; but Westley was a man of impulse and, as has been said, he was anxious to keep Proutt as a friend. Nevertheless, he had no sooner asked Proutt to take the dog than he regretted it, and hoped Proutt would refuse. But the dog trainer only gave a moment to slow consideration, with downcast eyes.

Then he said huskily: "I charge fifty dollars."

"Sure," said Westley.

"He's a well-blooded dog," said Proutt. "I'll come tomorrow and fetch him."

And with no further word—they were outside the store—he drove away. Westley, watching him go, was filled with vague disquiet. He wished he might withdraw; he wished Proutt would change his mind; he wished the trainer might not come next day. . . .

But Proutt did come, and Westley himself bade Reck into the trainer's buggy and watched the dog ride away with wistful eyes turned backward.

Westley's wife was more concerned than he; and he forgot his own anxiety in reassuring her.

## II

There are a thousand methods for the training of a bird dog, and each man prefers his own. There are some dogs which need much training; there are others which require little or none.

Reck was so nobly blooded that the instincts of his craft were deeply bedded in him. On his first day in the alder swamps with Proutt he proved himself to the full. Proutt was a dog beater, as all men know, but he did not beat dogs which obeyed him, and he did not beat Reck. This first day he was merely trying the dog.

Reck found a bird, and took stanch point, steady as a rock. It was not yet October, the season was not yet open; and so Proutt had no right to shoot. Nevertheless he did walk up this bird, and flushed it from where it lay six feet before Reck's nose, and knocked it over before it topped the alders.

Reck stood at point till the bird rose; when its whistling wings lifted it, his nose followed it upward, followed its fall. . . . But he did not stir, did not break shot; and Proutt, watching, knew that this was indeed a dog.

When the bird had fallen, Proutt said softly: "Reck! Fetch dead bird."

Now, this is in some measure the test of a setter. There are many setters which take a natural point and hold it; there are some few which are also natural retrievers, without training. Reck had been taught by Westley's children to fetch sticks or rocks at command. He knew the word.

He went swiftly forward and brought the woodcock, scarce ruffled, and laid it in Proutt's hand. And Proutt took the bird, and stood still, looking down at Reck with a darkly brooding face. Considering, weighing. . . . After a little he began to curse softly, under his breath; and he turned and stamped out of the alder run, and bade Reck to heel, and went home. And Reck trotted at his heels, tongue out, panting happily. . . .

There are many ways by which the Devil may come at a man. One of them is through hatred, and another way is to put a helpless thing in that man's hands. If the good in him outweighs the bad, well enough; but if the evil has ascendancy, then that man is utterly lost and damned.

Proutt hated Westley; Proutt had in his hands Reck, a dog by Westley well-beloved. And Reck was pliant in Proutt's hands, both because Proutt knew dogs and because Reck was by nature tractable, eager to please, anxious to do that which he was asked to do. The combination presented itself to Proutt full clearly, as he walked his homeward way that day, and it is to be supposed that he fought out what fight there was within himself, during that long walk, and through the evening that followed.

That Proutt had some battle with himself cannot be denied. No man sets out to destroy a soul without first overcoming the scruples which bind him; and there were scruples in Proutt. There must have been. He loved dogs, loved fine dogs, and Reck was fine. Yet the destruction of

Reck's honor and reputation and life—these were the ends which Proutt set himself to bring about—at what pain to his own heart no man may fully guess. It can only be known that in the end his hatred outweighed all else—that he threw himself into the thing he meant to do.

Reck, as has been shown, needed no training for his appointed work. Yet Proutt kept him, labored with him daily, for close to four long weeks, as all Fraternity men knew. None saw that training. It was known that Proutt took Reck far over the Sheepscot Ridge, where farms were all deserted, and no man was like to come upon him. But he had done that with dogs before, for woodcock lay thick in Sheepscot Valley. Once or twice men heard the barking of a dog in that valley; and there was a measure of pain in the notes. And three times men met Proutt driving homeward, with Reck lying weary and subdued upon the floor of the buggy, scarce fit to lift his head. It was remarked that Proutt was more dour and morose than ever; and Lee Motley thought the man was aging. . . .

One man only, and that man Jim Saladine, caught some inkling of that which was afoot. Jim was a deer hunter; and toward mid-October, with a shotgun under his arm for luck's sake, but never a buckshot in his cartridge pocket, he went one day into the Sheepscot Valley to search out the land. Deer lay in the swamps there; and Jim sought to locate them against the coming season. He moved slowly and quietly, as his custom was; ears and eyes open. And he saw many things which another man would never have seen.

Two things he saw which had significance. Once, in a muddy patch along the Sheepscot's brim, he came upon a deer's track; and other tracks beside it. A man's track, and a dog's.

Jim studied these tracks. They were sadly muddled; and he could make little of them. But he was sure of this much—that man and dog had been attentive to the tracks of the deer. And this stayed in Jim's mind, because no dog in Fraternity has any business with the track of a deer, and no man may justly set a dog upon such track.

Later that day Jim was to find some explanation for what he had seen. Where Fuller's brook comes into the Sheepscot, there lies an open meadow half a mile long, and half as broad; and near the lower end of the meadow half a dozen alders group about a lone tree in the open. Deer and moose, coming up the Sheepscot Valley, are like to cross the stream below and then traverse this meadow; and Jim Saladine stopped under cover at the meadow's head—it was near dusk—to see what he should see.

He saw what you may see any day along the Sheepscot, and what, by the same token, you may go a weary year without seeing. He saw a deer, a proud buck, come up from the stream and follow the meadow toward where he lay. It passed the isolated alder clump, and something there gave it alarm; for Jim saw its head lift—saw then the quick leap and rush which carried the creature to cover and away. . . .

Saw something else. Out from the alder clump burst a man, driving before him a dog. Dusk was falling, Jim could see their figures only dimly. But this much he saw. The man urged the dog after the deer, with waving arms; and the dog, ever looking backward shame-facedly, trotted slowly off upon the trail, the man still urging from behind.

They slipped into the brush where the deer had gone, and Jim caught no further glimpse of them.

Now, Saladine was an honest man, who loved the deer he hunted; and he was angry. But he was also a just man; and he could not be sure whom he had seen. So it was that he kept a still tongue, and waited, and through the weeks that followed he watched, patiently enough, for what should come.

He meant, in that hour, to take a hand.

## III

With a week of October left, Proutt took Reck home to Westley. Westley was not there, but Mrs. Westley marked Proutt's lowering eye, and was frightened of the man, and told Westley so when he came. But Westley was well enough pleased to have Reck back again; and he bade her forget Proutt.

Proutt had been, thus far, somewhat favored by fortune. The business of his office had taken Westley away from Fraternity for two weeks at a time, so that Proutt had had full time to do with Reck as he chose. Fraternity knew nothing of what had happened, though Jim Saladine may have guessed. There was one night at Will's store when Jim and Proutt were near fisticuffs. Proutt had brought Dan with him to the store; and Jim, studying the surly dog, asked:

"Dan ever notice a deer, Proutt?"

Proutt exclaimed profanely. "No," he said.

"I was over in the Sheepscot, t'other day," said Jim evenly. "See tracks where a dog had been after a deer."

"More like it was one of these setters," Proutt declared, watching them all from beneath lowered lids. "They'll kill a deer, or a sheep, give 'em a chance."

"It was hound's tracks," Jim persisted mildly; and something in Jim's tone, or in Proutt's own heart, made the trainer boil into fury, so that he strode toward Saladine. But Will Bissell came between, and the matter passed.

Proutt, before this, had taken Reck home; and the Westleys made much of the dog. Reck had affable and endearing little tricks of his own. He had a way of giving welcome, drawing back his upper lip so that his teeth showed as though in a snarl, yet panting with dog laughter all the time; and he had a way of talking, with high whines of delight, or throaty growls that ran the scale. And he would lie beside Westley, or beside Westley's wife, and paw at them until they held his paw in their hands, when he would go contentedly enough to sleep.

They thought the dog was unhappy when he came home to them. He had a slinking, shamed way about him. At first Westley supposed Proutt had whipped him; but Reck showed no fear of a whip in Westley's hands.

After two or three days this furtiveness passed away and Reck was the joyously affectionate creature he had always been. So the Westleys forgot his first attitude of guilt, and loved him ardently as men and women will love a dog.

Westley had opportunity for one day's hunting with him, and Reck never faltered at the task to which he had been born and bred.

He had one fault. Chained, he would bark at the least alarm, in a manner to wake the neighborhood. So Westley had never kept him chained. It was not the way of Fraternity to keep dogs in the house of nights; so Reck slept in the woodshed, and Westley knocked a plank loose and propped it, leaving Reck an easy avenue to go out or in. It was this custom of Westley's which gave Proutt the chance for which he had laid his plans.

October had gone; November had come. This was in the days when woodcock might be shot in November if you could find them. But most men who went into the woods bore rifles; for it was open season for deer. Now and then you might hear the snapping crash of a thirty-thirty in Whitcher Swamp, or at one of the crossings, or—if you went so far—in the alder vales along the Sheepscot. And one day in the middle of the month, when the ground was frozen hard, Proutt came to Nick Westley's home.

He came at noon, driving his old buggy. Westley was at dinner when he heard Proutt drive into the yard; and he went to the door and bade the dog trainer come in. But Proutt shook his head, and his eyes were somber.

"You come out, Westley," he said. "I've a word for you."

There was something in Proutt's tone which disturbed Westley. He put on his mackinaw, and drew his cap down about his ears, and went out into the yard. Reck had been asleep on the doorstep when Proutt appeared; he had barked a single bark. But now he was gone into the shed, out of sight; and when Westley came near Proutt's buggy, the dog trainer asked:

"Did you see Reck sneak away?"

Westley was angry; and he was also shaken by a sudden tremor of alarm. He said hotly enough: "Reck never sneaks. He did not sneak away."

"He knows I saw him," said Proutt. "He heard me yell."

Westley asked, with narrowing eyes: "What are you talking about? Where did you see him?"

"This morning," Proutt declared. "Scant daylight. Down in the Swamp."

Westley stood very still, trying to remember whether he had seen Reck early that morning. And he could only remember, with a shocking certainty, that Reck had not been at home when he came out of the house to do his chores. He had called and got no answer; and it may have been half an hour before the dog appeared. It had disturbed Westley at the time; and he scolded Reck for self-hunting. But any dog will range the home farm in the morning hours, and Westley had not taken the matter seriously.

Proutt's words, and his tone more than his words, made the matter very serious indeed. Westley forced himself to ask: "What were you doing in the Swamp?"

"I was after a deer," said Proutt; and when Westley remained silent, Proutt added huskily: "So was Reck."

Westley cried: "That's a lie." But his own voice sounded strange and unnatural in his ears. He would not believe. Yet he knew that other dogs had chased deer in the past, and would again. He had himself shot half a dozen. It was the law; and he was the instrument of the law. And this was the very bitterness of Proutt's accusation; for if it were true, then he must shoot Reck. And Westley would as soon have shot one of his own blood as the dog he loved.

In the little instant of silence that followed upon his word, he saw all this, too clearly. And in spite of his love for Reck, and in spite of his ardent longing to believe that Proutt had lied, he feared desperately that the man spoke truth. Westley's wife would never have believed; for a woman refuses to believe any evil of those she loves. She is loyal by refusing to believe; a man may believe and be loyal still.

Westley did not know whether to believe or not; but he knew that he was terribly afraid. He told Proutt: "That's a lie!" And Proutt, after a long moment, clucked to his horse and started on. Westley called after him: "Wait!"

Proutt stopped his horse; and Westley asked: "What are you going to do?"

"You're game warden," Proutt told him sullenly. "Nobody around here can make you do anything, less'n you're a mind to. But I've told you what's going on."

Westley was sweating in the cold, and said pitifully: "Proutt, are you sure?"

"Yes," said Proutt; and Westley cried: "What did you see?"

"I had a deer marked," said Proutt slowly. "He'd been feeding under an old apple tree down there. I was there before day this morning, figuring to get a shot at him. Crep' in quiet. Come day, I couldn't see him. But after a spell I heard a smashing in the brush, and he come out through an open, and was away before I could shoot. And hot after him came Reck."

"How far away?" Westley asked.

"Not more'n ten rod."

"You couldn't be sure."

"Damn it, man, I know Reck. Besides, I wouldn't want to say it was him, would I? He's a grand dog."

"What did you do?" Westley asked.

"Yelled at him to come in."

"Did he stop?"

"Stopped for one look, and then one jump into the brush and away he went."

Westley was almost convinced; he turned to call Reck, with some curious and half-formed notion that he might catechize the dog himself.

But when he turned, he found Reck at his side; and the setter was standing steadily, legs stiff and proud like a dog on show, eyes fixed on Proutt. There was no guilt in his attitude; nor was there accusation. There was only steady pride and self-respect; and Westley, at sight of him, could not believe this damning thing.

He said slowly: "Look at him, Proutt. If this were true, he'd be ashamed, and crawling. You saw some other dog."

Proutt shook his head. "He's a wise, bold dog, is Reck. Wise as you and me. He'll face it out if he can."

Westley pulled himself together, dropping one hand on Reck's head. "I don't believe it, Proutt," he said. "But I'm going to make sure."

"I am sure," said Proutt. "You can do as you please. But don't ask me to keep my mouth shut. You was quick enough to shoot Jackson's dog when you caught her on that doe."

"I know," said Westley; and his face was white. "I'll be as quick with Reck, when I'm sure."

"You'll take pains not to get sure."

Westley held his voice steady. "Did you ever have to call Reck off deer tracks?"

"No."

"Then he's never been taught not to run them?"

"Neither had Jackson's dog."

"What I mean," said Westley, "is this. He doesn't know it's wrong to run deer."

"That's no excuse."

"I'm not excusing him."

Proutt swore. "Well, what are you doing?"

"I'm going to take him into the swamp and find a deer," said Westley slowly. "See what he does. He's never been taught not to run them. So he'll run any that we find. If it's in him to do it, he'll take after them—"

Proutt nodded; and there was a certain triumph in his eyes. "You take your gun along," he said. "You're going to need that gun."

Westley, white and steady, said: "I'll take the gun. Will you come along?"

"Sure."

"Do you know where we can find a deer?"

"No; not this time o' day."

Westley turned toward the house. "Wait," he said. "I'll get my gun; and we'll go pick up Jim Saladine. He'll know."

Proutt nodded. "I'll wait," he agreed.

Westley went into the house. Reck stood on the doorstep. Proutt, waiting, watched Reck with a flickering, deadly light in his sullen eyes.

## IV

Saladine listened silently to Westley's request; but he looked at Proutt with an eye before which Proutt uneasily turned away his head. Nevertheless, being by nature a taciturn man, he made no comment or suggestion. He only said: "I can find a deer."

"Where?" Westley asked.

"Over in the Sheepscot," said Saladine. "I've got mine for this season; but I know some hardwood ridges over there where they're like to be feeding, come evening."

Proutt said uneasily: "Hell, there's a deer nearer than Sheepscot."

"Where?" Westley asked.

"Everywhere."

"We ain't got time to cover that much territory to-day," the hunter said mildly. "If the Sheepscot suits, I'll go along. I'm most sure we'll pick up deer."

Westley asked: "Do you think I'm testing Reck fair?"

Saladine spat. "Yes, I'd say so," he agreed.

"I've got work to do," Proutt still objected. "Sheepscot's a danged long way."

"I want you to come," said Westley.

So Proutt assented at last; and they set off in his team. He and Westley in the front seat, Saladine and Reck behind. A five-mile drive over the Sheepscot Ridge. "Past Mac's Corner," Saladine told them; and they went that way.

The road took them by Proutt's house; and old Dan, Proutt's hound, came out to bark at them, and saw Proutt, and tried to get into the buggy. Proutt bade him back to the house; then, as an afterthought, got out and shut the hound indoors. "Don't want him following," he said.

Saladine's eyes were narrow with thought, but he made no comment, and they moved on their way.

That part of Maine in which Fraternity lies is a curious study for geologists. A good many centuries ago, when the great glaciers graved this land, they slid down from north to south into the sea, and in their sliding plowed deep furrows, so that the country is cut up by ridges, running almost true north and south, and ending in peninsulas with bays between. Thus the coast line is jagged as a saw.

These ridges run far up into the State; and the Sheepscot Ridge is as bold as any one of them. There is no break in it; and it herds the little waterways down into Sheepscot River, and guides the river itself south till it meets the sea. There are trout in Sheepscot; and thirty years ago the valley was full of farms and mills; but these farms are for the most part deserted now, and the mills are gone, leaving only shattered dams to mark the spots where they stood. The valley is a tangle of second-growth timber, broken here and there by ancient meadows through which brooks meander. Here dwells every wild thing that the region knows.

Proutt's old buggy climbed the long road up the eastern slope of the ridge; and the somber beauty of the countryside lay outspread behind them. The sun was falling lower; the shadows were lengthening; and a cold wind blew across the land. Across George's Valley and George's Lake lay the lower hills, the Appleton Ridge beyond, and far southeast the higher domes of Megunticook and the Camden Hills. The bay itself could not be seen, but the dark top of Blue Hill showed, twenty miles beyond the bay; and Mount Desert, ten miles farther still. . . .

The men had no eyes for these beauties. They rode in silence, watching the road ahead. And they passed through Liberty, and past Mac's Corner, and so up to top the ridge at last. Paused there to breathe Proutt's horse.

Back at Proutt's home, about the time they were in Liberty, some one had opened the door of the shed in which old Dan was locked; and the hound, watching his chance, scuttled out into the open. What well-founded habit prompted him can only be guessed; certain it is that he wheeled, never heeding the calls from behind him, and took the road by which Proutt had gone, hard on his master's trail.

If the dog trainer had known this, matters might have turned out differently. But Proutt could not know.

## V

The roads from Sheepscot Ridge down into Sheepscot Valley are for the most part rough and little used. An occasional farmer comes this way; an occasional fisherman drops from the steep descent to the bridge. But the frost has thrown boulders up across the road; and grass grows between the ruts, and the young hardwood crowds close on either side. Down this road, at Saladine's direction, Proutt turned; and the westering sun shone through the leafless branches and laid a bright mosaic before the feet of the horse.

Halfway down the hill Saladine spoke. "Let's light out," he said. "We'll find something up along this slope."

Westley nodded; and Proutt, after a moment's hesitation, stopped his horse. They got out, and Reck danced about their feet. Proutt tied the horse to a sapling beside the road; and they climbed the ruined stone wall and turned into the wood. Westley alone had a gun; the others were unarmed.

The course Saladine set for them was straight along the slope, moving neither up nor down; and the three men, accustomed to the woods, went quickly. Westley spoke to Reck now and then. His only word was the hunter's command. "Get in there," he said. "Get in. Go on." And Reck ranged forward, and up, and down, covering a front of half a dozen rods as they advanced. Westley was in the middle, Saladine was below, Proutt above the other two.

Westley had suggested putting his hunting bell on Reck; but Proutt negatived that with a caustic word. "He'd know, then, you wanted birds," he said. "And, anyways, it'd scare the deer." So they followed the dog by sight or by the stirring of his feet among the leaves; and at times he was well ahead of them, and at times when he moved more slowly they were close upon his heels. At such moments Westley held them back till Reck should work ahead.

Whether Reck had any knowledge of what was in their minds, no man can say. There were moments when they saw he was uncertain, when he turned to look inquiringly back at them. But for the most part he worked steadily back and forth as a good dog will, quartering the ground by inches. And always he progressed along the ridge, and always they followed him. And Saladine, down the slope, watched Proutt as they moved on.

No man spoke, save that Westley urged Reck softly on when the dog turned back to look at them. And at the last, when he saw that Reck had found game, it needed no word to bring the three together, two or three rods behind the dog.

Reck, as the gunners say, was "marking game." Nose down, he moved forward, foot by foot; and now and then he stopped for long seconds motionless, as though at point; but always he moved forward again. And Westley felt the cold sweat upon his forehead; and he looked at Proutt and saw the dog trainer licking his tight lips. Only Saladine kept a steady eye upon the dog and searched the thickets ahead.

After a rod or two Reck stopped, and this time he did not move. And Westley whispered to the others: "Walk it up, whatever it is. Move in." So the men went slowly forward, eyes aching with the strain of staring into the shadows of the wood.

When Reck took his point he was well ahead of them. He held it while they came up beside him; and then, as they passed where the dog stood, something plunged in the brush ahead, and they all saw the swift flash of brown and the bobbing white tail as a buck deer drove straight away from them along the slope. And Proutt cried triumphantly:

"A deer, by God! I said it. I told you so. Shoot, Westley. Damn you, shoot!"

Westley stood still as still, and his heart was sunk a hundred fathoms deep. His hand was shaking and his eyes were blurred with tears. For Reck, who had no rightful concern with anything that roved the woods save the creatures which go on the wing, had marked a deer. Enough to damn him! Had hunted deer! . . .

He tried to lift the gun, but Saladine spoke sharply. "Hold on. Look at the dog. He didn't chase the deer."

Westley realized then that Reck was, in fact, still marking game, moving slowly on ahead of them. But Proutt cried: "He'd smelled it; he didn't see it go. Or there's another ahead."

"He didn't chase the deer," said Saladine. Westley, without speaking, moved forward behind the dog. And of a second his heart could beat again.

For they came to where the buck had been lying, to his bed, still warm. And Reck passed over this warm bed, where the deer scent was so strong the men could almost catch it themselves; passed over this scent as though it did not exist, and swung, beyond, to the right, and up the slope. The buck had gone forward and down.

"He's not after deer," said Saladine.

They knew what he was after in the next instant; for wings drummed ahead of them, and four partridges got up, huge, fleeting shadows in the darkening woods. And Reck's nose followed them in flight till they were gone, then swung back to Westley, wrinkling curiously, as though he asked:

"Why did you not shoot?"

Westley went down on his knees and put his arms about the dog's neck; and then he came to his feet uncertainly as Proutt exclaimed: "Hell, he was after deer. He knew we were watching. Took the birds."

Westley tried to find a word, but Saladine, that silent man, stepped forward.

"Westley," he said, "wait a minute. You, Proutt, be still."

They looked at him uncertainly, Proutt growling. And Saladine spat on the ground as though he tasted the unclean. "I've kept my mouth shut. Wanted to see. Meant to tell it in the end. Westley, Proutt broke your dog."

Westley nodded. "Yes." He looked at Proutt.

"He broke him to run deer."

Westley began to tremble, and he could not take his eyes from Saladine; and Proutt broke out in a roaring oath, till Saladine turned slowly upon him.

The deer hunter went on: "I waited to see. I knowed what would come; but I wanted to see. A bird dog's bred to birds. If he's bred right, it's in him. Reck's bred right. You can make him run deer. Proutt did. But you can't make him like it. Birds is his meat. You saw that just now. He didn't pay any heed to that buck; but he did pay heed to the pa'tridge."

Proutt cried: "Damn you, Saladine, you can't say a thing like that."

Saladine cut in: "I saw you. Month ago. Down by Fuller's Brook. A deer crossed there, up into the meadow. You was in the alders with Reck, and you tried to set him on. He wouldn't run, and you drove him. I saw you, Proutt."

Westley looked down at Reck; and he looked at Proutt, the trainer; and he looked back at Reck again. There was something in Reck's eyes which made him hot and angry; there was a pleading something in Reck's slowly wagging tail.... And Westley turned to Proutt, cool enough now; and he said:

"I can see it now, Proutt. I've known there was something, felt there was something." He laughed joyously. "Why, Proutt, you man who knows dogs. Didn't you know you could not kill the soul and the honor of a dog like mine? Reck is a thoroughbred. He knows his work. And you—"

He moved a little toward the other. "Proutt," he said, "I'm going to lick you till you can't stand."

Proutt's big head lowered between his shoulders. "So—" he said.

And Westley stepped toward him.

Saladine said nothing; Reck did not stir; and the woods about them were as still as still. It was in this silence, before a blow could be struck, that they heard the sound of running feet in the timber above them; and Saladine said swiftly: "Deer!"

He moved, with the word, half a dozen paces back by the way they had come, to an old wood road they had crossed, and stood there, looking up the slope. Westley and Proutt forgot each other and followed him; and Reck stayed close at Westley's heel. They could hear the beating feet more plainly now; and Saladine muttered:

"Scared. Something chasing it."

On the word, abruptly startling them, the deer came into view—a doe, running swiftly and unwearied. Striking the wood road, the creature followed the easier going, down the slope toward them; and because they were so still it failed to discover the men till it was scarce two rods away. Sighting them then, the doe stopped an instant, then lightly leaped into the brush at one side, and was gone.

The men did not look after the deer; they waited to see what pursued it. And after a moment Saladine's face grimly hardened, and Westley's became somber and grave, and Proutt turned pale as ashes.

For, lumbering down the hill upon the deer's hot trail, came Dan, that hound which Proutt had shut away at home—came Dan, hot on the trail as Proutt had taught him.

The dog saw them, as the deer had done, and would have swung aside. But Proutt cried, in a broken voice: "Dan, come in."

So came the hound to heel, sullenly and slowly, eyes off into the wood where the doe had gone; and for a moment no one spoke, till Saladine slowly drawled:

"Westley, give Proutt your gun."

Westley did not speak. He was immensely sorry for Proutt, and all his anger at the man had gone. Proutt looked old, and shaken, and weary; and he had dropped his heavy hand across Dan's neck. He caught Westley's eye and said harshly: "To hell with your gun. I'll use my own."

An instant more they stood; then Westley turned to Saladine. "Jim, let's go," he said. And Saladine nodded, and they moved away, Reck at Westley's heels. After a moment, an odd panic in his voice, Proutt called after them: "Wait, I'll ride you home."

But Saladine answered: "I'll walk!" And Westley did not speak at all. He and Reck and the deer hunter went steadily upon their way.

The sun was setting; and dark shadows filtered through the trees to hide old Proutt where he still stood close beside his dog.

## CHAPTER 13

# Sam

By Tom Hennessey

*EXCERPTED FROM* TOM HENNESSEY'S *BOOK* FEATHERS 'N FINS *(1989), THIS is the story of an English setter whose years of hunting grouse and woodcock covers in Maine earned him a permanent place in Tom's Gun Dog Hall of Fame. You'll see why in Tom's eloquent prose, which lets us witness and share the performance of a bird dog without equal.*

If you have a few minutes to spare, I'll tell you about Sam. When I brought the seven-week-old, tri-color English setter home in the spring of 1972, he was already displaying the merry manner and gentle disposition that is typical of his breed. His silky-white coat was sparsely ticked, and the black mask covering his eyes was dotted with tan eyebrows that gave him the appearance of being awake when he was asleep.

Two spears of hair tufted the top of his head, his ears were heavily feathered, and the tip of his lofty tail tossed as if keeping time with his brisk gait. A healthy and happy pup, for sure. And to my profound pleasure, he pointed everything that moved.

Because Sam was so "birdy" and easy to handle, I made the mistake of overtraining him. I realized it when he began pointing birds other than game species. Whenever we got into a cover where partridge or woodcock were scarce, he would start slamming onto stylish but unproductive points. The pup was, of course, trying to please me. I had worked him so often on planted pigeons that he figured whenever I hung a bell on him he'd best point something—and soon.

Fortunately, that wasn't a difficult problem to overcome. Whenever Sam's bell stopped, I could tell by his attitude whether he was telling the truth. If he wasn't, I'd walk away and command, "All right, Sam!" which would start him hunting again. It didn't take him long to realize I wasn't interested in his ruses and poses, no matter how impressive he looked.

Compared with my pointer Jake, Sam was a gentleman. It wasn't in his nature to be biggest and boldest or fastest or first, but somehow he usually managed to come out equal, if not ahead of his kennel mate. By no stretch of the imagination did the close-working setter have the flash and dash or the full-choke nose of the far-ranging pointer. But day in and day out, Sam showed me more birds than I could shoot, and when we returned home I wasn't hoarse and threatening to put an ad in the paper.

Sam was seven months old when his first hunting season arrived. At that time, woodcock were legal game on September 24. Naturally, the foliage hadn't given a thought to thinning out, and although the mornings steamed with melting frost, the covers swarmed with mosquitoes. It was so warm that by late morning we looked as if we were on the last leg of the Bataan Death March. Woodcock, however, were plentiful. Native woodcock—young of the year that had never heard a dog's bell, and held like they were glued to the ground.

Because I was working nights, Sam and I were able to hunt every day. He was young and I was younger, which means weather made no difference. Hot or cold, rain or shine, we scoured the covers. I have no idea how many birds the precocious pup accounted for in his first season. Let's just say that when the last day rolled around he was no longer a novice.

By the time he had a couple of years under his collar, Sam had become a seasoned campaigner. As tough as he was gentle, frequent encounters with thorns, broken glass, barbed wire, and Jake never dampened his desire. Nor did being struck by a car or tangling with a porcupine. The latter resulted in two operations and a week at the vet's.

Once in a while he'd have an off day, but I always figured he'd earned it. For the most part, though, he was steadfast and dependable, a journeyman who'd paid his dues, knew his trade, and accomplished his tasks without flourishes or fanfare. Hunting with him was like being in a canoe with a person who knows how to paddle.

During Sam's younger years, partridges seemed to be at the peak of their cycle. Seldom did we go into a cover without finding at least one. That, of course, was the reason he became skilled at handling the wild and wary birds. I shot more of them over his points than I have over any other dog's. Early on, the little setter learned that he couldn't crowd Ol' Ruff.

It was a pleasure just to watch him working a spooky partridge. He stalked like a cat—crouching, almost crawling. Slowly, he'd put out a foot, stealing each step. Often he'd draw back his paw when it first touched the ground, the way you pull back your hand when you're testing hot water. Those performances made the hair stand up on the back of my neck.

Sam hunted for fourteen years. To me, each of them was a gift as golden as October's uplands. Today, their memories are treasures. In his final hunting season, the old dog's eyesight and hearing were failing. Consequently, it was difficult for him to keep contact with me, and he often became confused and disoriented.

Age, however, doesn't diminish a hunting dog's spirit. The sound of a dog bell or the sight of a shotgun was all that was needed to start Sam leaping and romping like a pup. He reminded me of an over-the-hill fighter whose mind thinks he can, but whose body knows he can't. Rather than see him take a beating, I hung up his bell.

The hunting partner that I had raised from a pup was almost sixteen when, last July, I held him as he went to sleep. In a little cover not five minutes from my house, I deposited his ashes in the area where he pointed his last woodcock.

It may not surprise you to know that whenever I drive by there I see Sam's image glowing like a ghost in the shadowy alders. Stealing a step he is, with his ears cocked and his nostrils flared and his tail ramrod straight. And after I've driven past, I'll be damned if I don't feel the hair standing up on the back of my neck.

## CHAPTER 14

# The Sundown Covey

By Lamar Underwood

*THIS STORY WAS FIRST PUBLISHED IN 1973 IN THE AMWELL PRESS STORY COL-lection,* Hunting Moments of Truth. *This was a companion volume to* Fishing Moments of Truth, *where I had the opportunity to show that the big ones don't always get away. In the experience remembered here, the pointer dog Mack shared a hunt that turned out to be one for the books—literally.*

Nobody ever used the name "Sundown Covey" really. But it was the covey of bobwhite quail that we always looked for, almost with longing, as we turned our hunt homeward in the afternoon. By the time we came to that last stretch of ragged corn and soybean fields where this covey lived, the pines and moss-draped oaks would be looming darkly in the face of the dying sun. The other events of the afternoon never seemed to matter then. Tired pointer dogs bore ahead with new drive; we would watch carefully as they checked out each birdy objective, sure that we were headed for a significant encounter before we reached the small lane that led to the Georgia farmhouse. I always chose to think of those birds as "the sundown covey," although my grandfather or uncle usually would say something like "Let's look in on that bunch at the end of the lane." And then, more times than not, the evening stillness would be broken by my elder's announcement, "Yonder they are!" and we would move toward the dogs on point—small stark-white figures that always seemed to be chiseled out of the shadowy backdrop against the evening swamp.

There's always something special about hunting a covey of quail that you know like an old friend. One covey's pattern of movements between fields and swampy sanctuaries can be an intriguing and baffling problem. Another may be remarkably easy to find, and yet always manages to rocket away through such a thick tangle that you've mentally colored them gone, even before your finger touches the trigger. Another might usually present a good covey shot, while the singles tear away to . . . the backside of the moon, as far as you've been able to tell. My best hunts on more distant but greener pastures somehow have never seemed as inwardly satisfying as a day when a good dog and I can spend some time on familiar problems like these. Give me a covey I know, one that has tricked me, baffled me, eluded me—and by doing so brought me back to its corner of the woods for years.

In this sense, the covey we always hunted at sundown was even more special. As the nearest bunch of birds to the house, it was the most familiar. Here, trembling puppies got onto their first points. A lad learned that two quick shots into the brownish blur of the covey rise would put nothing into his stiff new hunting coat. A man returning from a war saw the birds running quick-footed across the lane and knew that he really was home again. The generations rolled on through times of kerosene lamps and cheap cotton to Ed Sullivan and soil-bank subsidies. And that same covey of bobwhites that had always seemed a part of the landscape still whistled in the long summer afternoons and hurtled across dead cornstalks that rattled in the winter breezes.

The hunters who looked for that covey and others in the fields nearby disciplined themselves never to shoot a covey below six birds. That number left plenty of seed for replenishment, so that every fall the coveys would again number fifteen to thirty birds, depending on how they had fared against predators.

Eventually, all that acreage moved out of our family. My visits to those coveys became less frequent as I necessarily turned toward education and then fields of commerce that were far away. But even during some marvelous quail-hunting days in other places, I often longed for return hunts to those intriguing coveys of the past. Would the swamp covey by the old pond still be up to their usual trick of flying into the field in the afternoon? Where would the singles from the peafield covey go now? Would the sundown covey still be there?

Finally, not long ago, the opportunity came for me to knock about a bit down in the home county. Several hunts with friends seemed as mere preludes to the long-awaited day when I got a chance to slip away alone to the old home grounds.

A soft rain had fallen during the night, but when I parked the truck by a thicket of pines just after sunrise, a stiff breeze had started tearing the overcast apart, and patches of blue were showing through the dullness. Shrugging into my bird vest, I ignored the shufflings and impatient whines that sounded from the dog box and stood a moment looking across a long soybean field that stretched toward a distant line of pines. I was mentally planning a route that would take me in a big circle to a dozen or so familiar coveys, then bring me to the sundown covey in the late evening. I unlatched the dog box, and the pointer, Mack, exploded from the truck and went through a routine of nervous preliminaries. I did the same, checking my bulging coat for shells, lunch and coffee. Then I clicked the double shut and stepped into the sedge alongside the field, calling: "All right, Mack. Look around!"

The pointer loped away in that deceptive, ground eating gait that was his way of going. At age four, he had not exactly developed into the close worker I had been wanting. His predecessors who had run these fields in decades before were big going speedsters suited to those times. Controlled burning and wide-roaming livestock kept the woodlands open then. Now most of the forests were so choked with brush and vines that wide-working dogs brought a legacy of frustration. Mack was easy to handle but tended to bend out too far from the gun unless checked back frequently. I really hated hearing myself say "Hunt close!" so often, but I hated even worse those agonizing slogging searches when he went on point in some dark corner of the swamp a quarter-mile from where I thought he'd been working.

The sun was bright on the sedge and pines now, and the air winy crisp after the rain. Mack was a bouncing flash of white as he worked through the sedge and low pines. Once he started over the fence into the field, but I called him back. I wanted him to keep working down the edge. While the bean field seemed like a tempting place to catch a breakfasting bevy, the cover bordering it had much better chances—at least three to one, according to the quail hunting education I had received here as a youngster. I could still imagine the sound of my grandfather's voice as he preached:

"Never mind all them picture book covey rises in those magazines you read. It's only now and then you'll catch these old woods coveys in the open. Birds once had to range wide and root hard for their keep. Now all the work's done for 'em. Combines and corn pickers leave so much feed scattered in the field the birds can feed in a few minutes, then leg it back into the cover. That's where you want to work. First, if they haven't gone to feed, you're likely to find 'em. If they've walked into the field, the dog'll trail 'em out. If they've already been into the field and fed, you'll still find 'em. Only time you'll miss is when they've flown into the field and are still there."

I had seen this simple philosophy pay increasing dividends as the years wore on. As the cover became thicker and the coveys smarter, the clear shot had become a rare, treasured experience. To spend a lot of time working through the fields was to be a dreamer of the highest order.

Still in the cover, we rounded the end of the small field and headed up the other side. I was beginning to feel the bite of the day's first disappointment; Mack had picked up no scent at all. Where were they? This covey had always been easy to find. Maybe they had been shot out, I thought. Maybe the whole place has been shot out.

I decided to play out a hunch. I pulled down a rusty strand of fence and stepped out into the field. Mack leaped the wire and raced away at full gallop. Far downfield he turned into the wind and suddenly froze in one of the most dramatic points I've ever seen. I knew he was right on top of those birds, his body curved tautly, his tail arching. "Oh ho!" I said aloud. "So you beggars did fly to the field."

My strides lengthened and became hurried. I snapped the gun open and checked the shells in an unnecessary gesture of nervousness. Normally steady hands seemed to tremble a little and felt very thick and uncertain. My heartbeat was a thunderous throb at the base of my throat.

My tangled nerves and wire-taut reflexes scarcely felt the nudge of a thought that said, "Relax. You've done this before." The case of shakes I undergo every time I step up to a point makes it difficult to attach any importance to that idea. Covey-rise jitters are known to have only one cure: action.

On my next step, the earth seemed to explode. The air was suddenly filled with blurry bits and pieces of speeding fragments, all boring toward the pines that loomed ahead. I found myself looking at one particular whirring form, and when the stock smacked against my face, the gun bucked angrily. The brown missile was unimpressed. He faded into the swamp, along with a skyful of surviving kinsmen. My loosely poked second shot failed to drop a tail-ender.

*Mighty sorry gathering up of partridges,* I thought, using the expression that was my uncle's favorite on the occasions when we struck out on a covey rise. "Sorry, boy," I called to Mack, who was busy vacuuming the grass in a futile search for downed birds.

My elders would have thought that bevy's maneuver of flying out to the field was the lowest trick in the book. But now the practice had become so typical among smart southern Bobs that it was hardly worth lamenting.

I called Mack away from his unrewarding retrieve and headed after those singles. The woods ahead looked clear enough for some choice shooting if I could keep Mack close.

Thirty minutes later I emerged from those woods a frustrated, angry man. My estimate that the birds had landed in the grassy, open pinelands was about two hundred yards wrong. Instead they had sailed on into one of the thickest, darkest sweet-gum swamps I've ever cursed a bird dog in. It took Mack all of fifteen seconds to get lost, and when I found him on point after ten minutes of searching, I proceeded to put the first barrel into a gum tree and the second into a screen of titi bushes. Then the heebiegeebies really took over as I walked over two separate singles that jumped unannounced. Finally, Mack pointed again, but as I fought through the tearing clutches of briers and vines to get to him, I bumped another single, which I shot at without a glimmer of hope. That action caused Mack to take matters into his own hands and send the bird he was pointing vaulting away through the trees. Then followed a lot of unnecessary yelling, and we headed for the clear.

I should have known better. Single-bird hunting in that part of Georgia had become a sad business. Now I was discovering that my old hunting grounds were in the same shape as the rest of the county. If you were going to mess with singles, you had to wait for the right type of open woods. Most were just too thick to see a dog, much less a six-ounce bird. The day's shooting was certainly not going to follow the patterns of the past when it came to singles. I would have to wait until I got a bevy scattered in a better place.

We cut away from the field into a section of low moss-draped oak trees. Mack ranged ahead, working smartly. My frustrations of the first covey slipped away as I began considering the coming encounter with the next set of old friends. This covey, if they were still in business, would be composed of dark swamp birds that lived in the edge of the creek swamp but used this oak ridge to feed on acorns during early mornings and late afternoons. They were extremely hard to catch in the open, sometimes running for hundreds of yards in front of a dog on point. But what a sight they always made as they hurtled up among the moss-draped oaks on the lucky occasions when we did get them pinned nicely.

This oak ridge was fairly open, so I let Mack move on out a little bit. When he cut through one thickish cluster of trees and did not come out right away, I knew he had 'em.

*Incredible*, I thought. *The first two coveys are still here, and we've worked 'em both.* Then the words turned into brass in my mouth as I eased up to the dog and past him. The thunderous rise I had been expecting failed to occur. I let Mack move on ahead to relocate. Catlike, he crept through the low grass for a few yards, then froze again. I moved out in front once more, and still nothing happened.

Then, suddenly I heard them. Several yards out front the dry leaves rustled under the flow of quick-moving feet. The covey was up to its old trick of legging it for the sanctuary of the swamp.

I hurried forward, crashing through the briers. Just ahead, the low cover gave way to a wall of sweetgum and cypress that marked the beginning of the swamp. Too late! I caught the sound of wings whirring. The birds had made the edge and were roaring off through the trees. They seemed to get up in groups of two and three. I caught an occasional glimpse of dim blurs through the screen of limbs and snapped a shot at one. Leaves and sticks showered down as Mack raced forward. Seconds later he emerged from the brush carrying a plump rooster bobwhite.

Had you seen me grinning over that bird, you might have thought I hadn't scored in five years. But the shot seemed mighty satisfying under the conditions. A few moments like this could make the day a lot more glorious than a coatful of birds ever could.

Now we followed an old lane that led down across the swamp and out beside a tremendous cornfield surrounded by pine and gallberry flats. I expected to find a couple of coveys here—and did, too, as the morning wore on in a succession of encounters with my old friends. A heart-warming double from a bevy Mack pinned along a fence row was followed by a succession of bewildering misses when we followed the singles into an open gallberry flat where I should have been able to score. Then we had the fun of unraveling a particularly difficult relocation problem when Mack picked up some hot scent in the corn but could not trail out to the birds. The edge of the field sloped down to a grassy flat to an old pond with pine timber on the far side. I just knew those birds had flown across that pond to the woods to hole up for the day. When I took Mack over, he made a beautiful point, standing just inside the woods. I wish I could always dope out a covey like that.

We spent the middle of the day stretched out on the grass on the pond dam. The sandwiches and coffee couldn't have tasted better. The sun was warm and crows and doves flew against the blue sky. I thought about old hunts and old friends and couldn't have felt better.

In the afternoon we had a couple of interesting pieces of action but failed to find some of my old neighbor coveys at home. My thoughts kept reaching ahead to the late-afternoon time when I would near the old now-deserted house by the lane and see the sundown covey again. Surely they would still be there. After all, we had been finding most of the old coveys. Who says you can't go home again? Who's afraid of you, Thomas Wolfe?

The sun was dipping toward the pines and a sharp chill had come on when I skirted the last field and entered the stretch of open pine woods where I was counting on finding the covey of birds that I had carried in my mind all my life. Before I had gone 50 yards I had come on something that shocked me as though I'd walked up on a ten-foot rattlesnake. A newly cut stake had been driven in the ground, and a red ribbon tied to the top of it. Farther on there was another then another.

I had known that the new Savannah-Atlanta-Super-Highspeed-Interstate-Get-You-There-Quick Highway was to pass through this general area. But surely, a couple miles away. Not here. Not right here.

Gradually, my disbelief turned into anger. I felt like heading for the car right then and getting the hell out of there. Then suddenly three shots boomed in the woods some distance ahead.

Well, it was apparent that the sundown covey was still around. But an intruder had found them. I decided to go on up and talk to whoever it was. Actually, he probably had as much right to be here as I did now. I couldn't believe he was a regular hunter on this land though. The coveys I had been finding all day were too populous with birds to be gunned heavily.

I walked slowly through the pines for a few minutes without spotting the other hunter. Then his gun thudded again, this time from farther down in the swamp. He's after the singles now, I thought. I called in Mack and waited there opposite the swamp. The other fellow would have to come out this way.

During the next few minutes two more separate shots sounded. The sun sank lower, and the breeze blew harder in the pines. Finally, I heard the bushes shaking and a man came out of the cover. When Mack started barking he spotted me and headed my way. As he came up I saw that he was young, carried an automatic and wore no hunting coat. He had some quail by the legs in his left hand.

"Looks like you did some good," I said.

"Yea, I got six."

"Where's your dog?" I asked.

"Oh, I don't have a dog. I spotted a covey crossing the road down there by the lane. I had the gun in the truck, so I went after 'em. Got three when I flushed 'em and three more down in the branch. Tiny little covey, though. I don't think there were more than six when I first flushed 'em. I imagine people been framin' into this bunch all the time." My heart sank when he said that. I didn't know what to say. He paused a minute, looking at Mack. "That's a nice dog. He any good?"

"Fair," I said. "Maybe you shouldn't have done that."

"What?"

"Shoot a small covey on down that way."

"Don't mean nothing. There's always a covey of birds along here. Every year. But there won't be for long. Interstate's coming through."

"Yea," I said slowly. "I see it is."

"Well, I gotta run. That's sure a nice-looking dog, Mister. See you around."

I watched him walk away. Then I leaned back against a pine, listening to the swamp noises. The wings of a pair of roost-bound ducks whispered overhead. An owl turned up down in the swamp. Somehow I kept thinking that I would hear some birds calling each other back into a covey. Perhaps two or three had slipped away unseen from the roadside.

The night pressed down. I started for the truck.

Orion wheeled overhead by the time I opened the tailgate for Mack. I started thinking about some new places I wanted to try. I paused with my hand on the door, listening, hoping.

But never again did I hear that flutelike call that had sounded for me from that swamp so many times before.

# Sources

"The Road to Tinkhamtown," by Corey Ford, *Field & Stream*, June 1970. Reprinted with the permission of Dartmouth College Library.

"The Dog Man," by Gene Hill, *Tears and Laughter: A Couple of Dozen Dog Stories* (Los Angeles: Petersen Prints, 1981). All rights reserved. Reprinted by permission of Cathy Hill.

The stories "Homebodies," "A Drink for the Dog," and "Sam" by Tom Hennessey are all from the Tom Hennessey book *Feathers 'n Fins*, The Amwell Press, 1989, reprinted by permission of Nancy Hennessey.

"A Blue Ridge Hunt," by Christopher Camuto, excerpted from "Solitary in Winter," *Hunting from Home: A Year Afield in the Blue Ridge Mountains* (New York: W. W. Norton & Co., 2003). Reprinted by permission of W. W. Norton & Co.

"The Old Maid," by Havilah Babcock, *Tales of Quails 'n Such: A Collection of Hunting and Fishing Stories* (Columbia: University of South Carolina Press, 1985). Reprinted by permission of the University of South Carolina Press.

"The Family Honor," by Nash Buckingham, excerpted from *De Shootinest Gent'man and Other Tales* (New York: Derrydale Press, 1934). Editor's note: Like all Buckingham stories, "The Family Honor" appeared in a magazine before the book version, but the editor has been unable to find the exact spot.

"My Most Memorable Dog," by Archibald Rutledge, *Bird Dog Days, Wingshooting Ways*, edited by Jim Casada (Columbia: University of South Carolina Press, 2016). Reprinted by permission of Jim Casada.

"The Tail-Ender," by Henry P. Davis, originally appeared in *Outdoors* magazine, reprinted from *Outdoors Unlimited*, edited by J. Hammond Brown (New York: A. S. Barnes, 1947).

"Old Tantrybogus" and "Mine Enemy's Dog," by Ben Ames Williams, *Thrifty Stock and Other Stories* (New York: E. P. Dutton & Co., 1923).

"The Demon Dog of Deacon's Draw," by Jim Rikhoff, originally appeared in *American Rifleman*, reprinted from *Mixed Bag* (Clinton, NJ: Amwell Press, 1979). Reprinted by permission of Jim Rikhoff.

"The Sundown Covey," by Lamar Underwood, from *Hunting Moments of Truth*, Clinton, NJ: Amwell Press, 1973. Reprinted by permission.